Law Made Simple

Personal Legal
Forms
Simplified

Personal Legal Forms Simplified

by Daniel Sitarz
Attorney-at-Law

Nova Publishing Company
Small Business and Consumer Legal Books and Software
Carbondale, Illinois

ISBN 0-935755-97-7   Book w/CD   ($28.95)

Cataloging-in-Publication Data
    Sitarz, Dan, 1948-
        Personal Legal Forms Simplified / by Daniel Sitarz. -- 1st ed.
        256 p. cm. -- (Law Made Simple series). Includes index.
        1. Forms (Law)—United States—Popular Works. 2. Civil Law—United States—Forms.
        I. Sitarz, Daniel. II. Title. III. Series.
        ISBN 0-935755-97-7, Book/CD Set ($28.95).

Nova Publishing Company is dedicated to providing up-to-date and accurate legal information to the public. All Nova publications are periodically revised to contain the latest available legal information.

1st Edition; 1st Printing   December, 2003

This publication is designed to provide accurate and authoritative information in regard to the subject matter covered. It is sold with the understanding that the publisher and author are not engaged in rendering legal, accounting, or other professional services. If legal advice or other expert assistance is required, the services of a competent professional person should be sought.

—From a Declaration of Principles jointly adopted by a Committee of the American Bar Association and a Committee of Publishers

DISCLAIMER

Because of possible unanticipated changes in governing statutes and case law relating to the application of any information contained in this book, the author, publisher, and any and all persons or entities involved in any way in the preparation, publication, sale, or distribution of this book disclaim all responsibility for the legal effects or consequences of any document prepared or action taken in reliance upon information contained in this book. No representations, either express or implied, are made or given regarding the legal consequences of the use of any information contained in this book. Purchasers and persons intending to use this book for the preparation of any legal documents are advised to check specifically on the current applicable laws in any jurisdiction in which they intend the documents to be effective.

Nova Publishing Company
Small Business and Consumer Legal Books and Software
1103 West College Street
Carbondale, IL 62901
Editorial: (800) 748-1175

Distributed by:
National Book Network
4501 Forbes Blvd., Suite 200
Lanham, MD 20706
Orders: (800) 462-6420

Table of Contents

Introduction

This book is part of Nova Publishing Company's new *Law Made Simple* series. The various self-help legal guides in this series are prepared by licensed attorneys who feel that public access to the American legal system is long overdue.

Law in American society is far more pervasive than ever before. There are legal consequences to virtually every public and most private actions in today's world. Leaving knowledge of the law within the hands of only the lawyers in such a society is not only foolish, but dangerous as well. A free society depends, in large part, on an informed citizenry. This book and others in Nova's *Law Made Simple* series are intended to provide the necessary information to those members of the public who wish to use and understand the law for themselves.

However, in an area as wide-ranging as personal legal forms, encompassing topics as diverse as property law, constitutional law, marital law, wills, trusts, and legal contracts, it is not always prudent to attempt to handle every legal situation that arises without the aid of a competent attorney. Although the information presented in this book will give its readers a basic understanding of the areas of law covered, it is not intended that this text entirely substitute for experienced legal assistance in all situations. Throughout this book there are references to those particular situations in which the aid of a lawyer is strongly recommended.

Regardless of whether or not a lawyer is ultimately retained in certain situations, the legal information in this handbook will enable readers to understand the framework of law in this country and how to effectively use legal forms in their personal lives.

To try and make that task as easy as possible, technical legal jargon has been eliminated whenever possible and plain English used instead. Naturally, plain easy-to-understand English is not only perfectly proper for use in all legal documents but, in most cases, leads to far less confusion on the part of later readers. When it is necessary in this book to use a legal term that may be unfamiliar to most people, the word will be shown in *italics* and defined when first used.

CHAPTER 1
Using Legal Forms

American society operates on a daily assortment of legal forms. There are more legal forms in use in America than in any other country on Earth. Individuals are not immune to this flood of legal forms. The legal system in America has a profound impact on everyone. While large corporations are able to hire expensive lawyers to deal with their legal problems and paperwork, most individuals and families cannot afford such a course of action. Whether preparing a will, leasing a house, or selling a piece of personal property, individuals must deal with a variety of legal documents throughout their lives, usually without the aid of an attorney. Unfortunately, many people who are confronted with such forms do not understand the legal ramifications of the use of these forms. They simply sign the lease, contract, or bill of sale with the expectation that it is a fairly standard document without any unusual legal provisions. They trust that the details of the particular document will fall within what is considered generally acceptable. In most cases, this may be true. In many situations however, it is not. Our court system is clogged with cases in which two people are battling over what was the real intent of the incomprehensible legal language in a certain contract.

Much of the confusion over legal documents comes from two areas. First, there is a general lack of understanding among most people regarding the framework of contract law. Second, many legal documents are written in antiquated legal jargon that is difficult for most lawyers to understand and nearly impossible for an average person to comprehend. Although this book will provide an overview of the uses of legal contracts in many standard situations, it is not intended to be a complete reference on the subject of contract law.

The contracts and other various legal documents that are used in this book are, however, written in plain English. Standard legal jargon, as used in most lawyer-prepared documents, is, for most people, totally incomprehensible. Despite the lofty arguments by attorneys regarding the need for such strained and difficult language, the vast majority of legalese is absolutely unnecessary. Clarity, simplicity, and readability should be the goal in legal documents. In most contexts, "buyer" and "seller," "landlord" and "tenant," or some other straightforward term of definition of the parties involved is possible. Unfortunately, certain obscure legal terms are the only words that accurately and precisely describe some things in certain legal contexts. In those few cases, the unfamiliar legal term will be defined when first used. Generally, however, simple terms are used.

All of the legal documents contained in this book have been prepared in essentially the same manner that attorneys use to create legal forms. Many people believe that lawyers prepare each legal document that they use entirely from scratch. Nothing could be further from the truth. Invariably, lawyers begin their preparation of a legal document with a standardized legal form book. Every law library has multi-volume sets of these encyclopedic texts which contain blank forms for virtually every conceivable legal situation. Armed with these pre-prepared legal forms, in many cases, lawyers simply fill in the blanks and have their secretaries retype the form for the client. Of course, the client is generally unaware of this process.

This book provides individuals with a set of legal forms that have been prepared with the problems and normal transactions of everyday life in mind. These forms are intended to be used in those situations that are clearly described by the specific terms of the particular form. Of course, while most transactions will fall within the bounds of these normal situations, some legal circumstances will present non-standard situations. The forms in this book are designed to be readily adaptable to most usual situations. They may be carefully altered to conform to the particular transaction that you may be confronted with. However, if you are faced with a complex or tangled legal situation, the advice of a competent lawyer is highly recommended. It may also be advisable to create your legal document for a certain legal situation and have a lawyer check it for any local legal circumstances.

The proper and cautious use of the forms provided in this book will allow the typical person to save considerable money on legal costs. Perhaps more importantly, these forms will provide a method for the person to avoid costly misunderstandings about what exactly was intended in a particular situation or transaction. By using the forms provided to clearly set out the terms and conditions of everyday personal dealings, disputes over what was really meant can be avoided.

How to Use This Book

In each chapter of this book, you will find an introductory section that will give you an overview of the types of situations in which the forms in that chapter will generally be used. Following that overview, there will be a brief explanation of the specific uses for each form. Included in the information provided for each form will be a discussion of the legal terms and conditions provided in the form. Finally, for each form, there is a listing of the information that must be compiled to complete the form.

The preferable manner for using these forms is to use the enclosed Forms-on-CD. Please refer to the readme.doc file on the Forms-on-CD for specific instructions on completing the computer-ready forms. However, it is perfectly acceptable to prepare these forms directly from the book by making a copy of the form, filling in the information that is necessary, and then retyping the form in its entirety on clean white letter-sized paper.

For purposes of simplification, most of the forms in this book are set out as a form that would be used by two individuals. If businesses are parties to the contract, please identify the name and type of business entity (for example: Jackson Car Stereo, a New York sole proprietorship, etc.) in the first section of the contract. Many of the forms in this book have blanks for inserting the state or county. If you are a resident of Louisiana, substitute "parish" for "county." If you are a resident of Pennsylvania, Massachusetts, Virginia, or Kentucky, substitute "Commonwealth" for "state." If you are a resident of Washington D.C., please substitute "District of Columbia" for "state." In most cases, masculine and feminine terms have been eliminated and the generic "it" or "them" is used instead. In the few situations where this leads to awkward sentence construction, "his or her" or "he or she" may be used instead.

It is recommended that you review the table of contents of this book in order to gain a broad overview of the range and type of legal documents that are available. Then, before you prepare any of the forms for use, you should carefully read the introductory information and instructions in the chapter containing the particular form that you wish to use. Try to be as detailed and specific as possible as you fill in these forms. The more precise the description, the less likelihood that later disputes may develop over what was actually intended by the language chosen. The careful preparation and use of the legal forms in this book should provide the typical individual with most of the legal documents necessary for day-to-day life. If in doubt as to whether a particular form will work in a specific application, please consult a competent lawyer.

Personal Legal Forms Simplified Forms-on-CD

Quick-Start Installation for PC's:

1 Insert the enclosed CD in your computer.
2. The installation program will start automatically. Follow the onscreen dialogue and make your appropriate choices.
3 If the CD installation does not start automatically, click on START, then RUN, then BROWSE, and select your CD drive, and then select the file "Install.exe." Finally, click OK to run the installation program.
4. Open the "Readme.doc" document (which should be visible on your Windows desktop). Print out and follow instructions on the "Readme.doc" document.

Installation Instructions for MAC's:

1. Insert the enclosed CD in your computer.
2. Copy the folder "Personal Legal Forms for Macs" to your hard drive.
3. Open the folder and print out the "readme.doc" file.
4. Double-click on the file "acrobat reader installation.exe." This will install the Adobe Acrobat Reader program.
5. Follow the instructions on the Readme document.

CHAPTER 2
Contracts

The foundation of most agreements is a contract. A *contract* is merely an agreement by which two or more parties each promise to do something. This simple definition of a contract can encompass incredibly complex agreements. The objective of a good contract is to clearly set out the terms of the agreement. Once the parties have reached an oral understanding of what their agreement should be, the terms of the deal should be put in writing. Contrary to what many attorneys may tell you, the written contract should be clearly written and easily understood by both parties to the agreement. It should be written in precise and unambiguous terms. The most common causes for litigation over contracts are arguments over the meaning of the language used. Remember that both sides of the agreement should be able to understand and agree to the language being used.

A contract has to have certain prerequisites to be enforceable in court. These requirements are relatively simple and most will be present in any standard agreement. However, you should understand what the various legal requirements are before you prepare your own contracts. To be enforceable, a contract must have *consideration*. In the context of contract law, this simply means that both parties to the contract must have promised to do something or forego taking some type of action. If one of the parties has not promised to do anything or forego any action, he or she will not be able to legally force the other party to comply with the terms of the contract. There has to be some form of mutual promise for a contract to be valid. For example: Andy agrees to pay Bill if Bill paints a car. Andy's promise is to pay Bill if the job is completed. Bill's promise is to paint the car. If Bill paints the car and is not paid, Andy's promise to pay Bill can be enforced in court. Similarly, if Bill fails to paint the car, Andy can have the contract enforced in court. Andy and Bill's mutual promises are the consideration necessary to have a valid and enforceable contract.

Another requirement is that the parties to the contract be clearly identified and the terms of the contract also be clearly spelled out. The terms and description need not be complicated, but they must be spelled out in enough detail to enable the parties to the contract (and any subsequent court) to clearly determine what exactly the parties were referring to when they made the contract. In the prior example, the names and addresses of the parties must be included for the contract to be enforceable. In addition, a description of the car must be incorporated in the contract. Finally, a description of the type of paint job and the amount of money to be paid should also be contained in the contract.

The following documents are included for use in situations requiring a basic contract. There are documents for assigning, modifying, extending, and terminating a basic contract. A form for adding exhibits to a contract is also included. *Note*: If you are at all unsure of the correct use of any forms in this chapter, please consult a competent attorney.

Contract: This basic document can be adapted for use in many situations. The terms of the contract that the parties agree to should be carefully spelled out and inserted where indicated. The other information that is required are the names and addresses of the parties to the contract and the date the contract is to take effect. This basic contract form is set up to accommodate an agreement between two individuals. If a business is party to the contract, please identify the name and type of business entity (for example: Jackson Car Stereo, a New York sole proprietorship, etc.) in the first section of the contract.

Extension of Contract: This document should be used to extend the effective time period during which a contract is in force. The use of this form allows the time limit to be extended without having to entirely redraft the contract. Under this document, all of the other terms of the contract will remain the same, with only the expiration date changing. You will need to fill in both the original expiration date and the new expiration date. Other information necessary will be the names and addresses of the parties to the contract and a description of the contract. A copy of the original contract should be attached to this form.

Modification of Contract: Use this form to modify any other terms of a contract (other than the expiration date). The modification can be used to change any portion of the contract. Simply note what changes are being made in the appropriate place on this form. If a portion of the contract is being deleted, make note of the deletion. If certain language is being substituted, state the substitution clearly. If additional language is being added, make this clear. For example, you may wish to use language as follows:

- "Paragraph _____ is deleted from this contract."
- "The following new paragraph is added to this contract:"

A copy of the original contract should be attached to this form.

Termination of Contract: This document is intended to be used when both parties to a contract mutually desire to end the contract prior to its original expiration date. Under this form, both parties agree to release each other from any claims against each other based on anything in the contract. This document effectively ends any contractual arrangement between two parties. Information necessary to complete this form are the names and addresses of the parties to the contract, a description of the contract, and the effective date of the termination of the contract.

Assignment of Contract: This form is for use if one party to a contract is assigning its full interest in the contract to another party. This effectively substitutes one party for another under a contract. This particular assignment form has both of the parties agreeing to indemnify and hold each other harmless for any failures to perform under the contract while they were the party liable under it. This *indemnify and hold harmless* clause simply means that if a claim arises for failure to perform, each party agrees to be responsible for the period of their own performance obligations. A description of the contract which is assigned should include the parties to the contract, the purpose of the contract, and the date of the contract. Other information that is necessary to complete the assignment is the name and address of the *assignor* (the party who is assigning the contract), the name and address of the *assignee* (the party to whom the contract is being assigned), and the date of the assignment. A copy of the original contract should be attached to this form. A copy of a Consent to Assignment of Contract should also be attached, if necessary.

Consent to Assignment of Contract: This form is used if the original contract states that the consent of one of the parties is necessary for the assignment of the contract to be valid. A description of the contract and the name and signature of the person giving the consent are all that is necessary for completing this form. A copy of the original contract should be attached to this form.

Contract Exhibit: This form may be used with any contract. It provides a simple method for attaching other documents to the contract and having them considered as a legal part of the contract. If you have documents, letters, forms, etc. that you feel are necessary to have as a part of a contract, use this simple form. The space after "Exhibit" in the title of this document is for placing a letter to describe this exhibit (for example: Exhibit A). In the space provided, describe clearly which particular contract the exhibit is to be attached to (for example: The Contract dated June 1, 2004, between John Smith of 111 Main St., Uptown, NY and Mary Johnson of 222 Broadway Ave., Downtown, CA).

Contract

This Contract is made on _____ , 20 _____ ,

between _____ ,

address:

and _____ ,

address:

For valuable consideration, the parties agree as follows:

No modification of this Contract will be effective unless it is in writing and is signed by both parties. This Contract binds and benefits both parties and any successors. Time is of the essence of this contract. This document, including any attachments, is the entire agreement between the parties. This Contract is governed by the laws of the State of

_____ .

The parties have signed this Contract on the date specified at the beginning of this Contract.

_____   _____
Signature   Signature

_____   _____
Printed Name   Printed Name

Extension of Contract

This Extension of Contract is made on _____ , 20 _____ ,
between _____ ,
address:

and _____ ,
address:

For valuable consideration, the parties agree as follows:

1. The following described contract will end on _____ , 20 _____ :

    This contract is attached to this Extension and is a part of this Extension.

2. The parties agree to extend this contract for an additional period, which will begin immediately on the expiration of the original time period and will end on
    _____ , 20 _____ .

3. The Extension of this contract will be on the same terms and conditions as the original contract. This Extension binds and benefits both parties and any successors. This document, including the attached original contract, is the entire agreement between the parties.

The parties have signed this Extension on the date specified at the beginning of this Extension of Contract.

_____   _____
Signature   Signature

_____   _____
Printed Name   Printed Name

18

Modification of Contract

This Modification of Contract is made on _____ , 20 _____ ,
between _____ ,
address:

and _____ ,
address:

For valuable consideration, the parties agree as follows:

1. The following described contract is attached to this Modification and is made a part of this Modification:

2. The parties agree to modify this contract as follows:

3. All other terms and conditions of the original contract remain in effect without modification. This Modification binds and benefits both parties and any successors. This document, including the attached contract, is the entire agreement between the parties.

The parties have signed this Modification on the date specified at the beginning of this Modification of Contract.

_____   _____
Signature   Signature

_____   _____
Printed Name   Printed Name

Termination of Contract

This Termination of Contract is made on _____ , 20 _____ , between _____ , address:

and _____ , address:

For valuable consideration, the parties agree as follows:

1. The parties are currently bound under the terms of the following described contract, which is attached and is part of this Termination:

2. They agree to mutually terminate and cancel this contract effective on this date. This Termination Agreement will act as a mutual release of all obligations under this contract for both parties, as if the contract has not been entered into in the first place.

3. This Termination binds and benefits both parties and any successors. This document, including the attached contract being terminated, is the entire agreement between the parties.

The parties have signed this Termination on the date specified at the beginning of this Termination of Contract.

_____   _____
Signature   Signature

_____   _____
Printed Name   Printed Name

Assignment of Contract

This Assignment of Contract is made on _____ , 20 _____ ,
between _____ ,
address:

and _____ ,
address:

For valuable consideration, the parties agree to the following terms and conditions:

1. The Assignor assigns all interest, burdens, and benefits in the following described contract to the Assignee:

   This contract is attached to this Assignment and is a part of this Assignment.

2. The Assignor warrants that this contract is in effect, has not been modified, and is fully assignable. If the consent of a third party is necessary for this Assignment to be effective, such consent is attached to this Assignment and is a part of this Assignment. Assignor agrees to indemnify and hold the Assignee harmless from any claim which may result from the Assignor's failure to perform under this contract prior to the date of this Assignment.

3. The Assignee agrees to perform all obligations of the Assignor and receive all of the benefits of the Assignor under this contract. Assignee agrees to indemnify and hold the Assignor harmless from any claim which may result from the Assignee's failure to perform under this contract after the date of this Assignment.

4. This Assignment binds and benefits both parties and any successors. This document, including any attachments, is the entire agreement between the parties.

The parties have signed this Assignment on the date specified at the beginning of this Assignment of Contract.

_____   _____
Signature of Assignor   Signature of Assignee

_____   _____
Printed Name of Assignor   Printed Name of Assignee

Consent to Assignment of Contract

Date: _____ , 20 _____

To:_____

I am a party to the following described contract:

This contract is the subject of the attached Assignment of Contract.

I consent to the Assignment of this Contract as described in the attached Assignment, which provides that the Assignee is substituted for the Assignor.

_____
Signature

_____
Printed Name

Contract Exhibit _____

This Contract Exhibit _____ is attached and made part of the following contract:

CHAPTER 3
Signatures and Notary Acknowledgments

Signatures and notary acknowledgments for legal forms serve similar but slightly different purposes. Both are used to document the formal signing of a legal instrument, but the notarized acknowledgment also serves as a method of providing a neutral witness to the signature, and thus authenticates the signature. Also, a notarized acknowledgment can serve an additional purpose of providing a statement under oath. For example, a notarized acknowledgment can be used to assert that a person states, under oath, that he or she has read the document that he or she is signing and believes that what it contains is the truth.

The use of a notary acknowledgment is not required for all legal forms. The notary acknowledgments contained in this chapter are to be used only for the purpose of providing a notarization required for recording a document. Generally, notarization is only necessary if the document is intended to be recorded with an official government office in some manner. For example, all documents relating to the sale of real estate should be recorded in the county recorder's office or register of deeds office in the county (or parish) where the property is located. In virtually all jurisdictions, such documents must be notarized before they will be recorded. Similarly, some states require automobile titles and similar documents to be notarized. Check with your local county clerk to determine the requirements in your locale.

Another unofficial purpose of notarization of legal documents is to make the document seem more important to the parties. By formally having their signatures witnessed by a notary public, the parties are attesting to the fact that they ascribe a powerful purpose to the document. Although this type of notarization has no legal value, it does serve a valid purpose in solemnizing the signing of an important legal document.

For all of the notary acknowledgment forms contained in this chapter, the following information is necessary:

- The name of the state in which the document is signed
- The name of the county in which the document is signed
- The date when the document is signed
- The name of the person who is signing the document
- The name of the notary public (or similar official)
- The state where the notary is authorized to perform

- The county in which the notary is registered to act
- The date when the notary's commission will expire

In addition, many states require that the notary place an embossed seal on the document to authenticate the notarization process. The notary who completes the acknowledgment will know the correct procedure for your state.

A simple signature line merely serves to provide a place for a party to a document to sign his or her name. However, care must be taken to be sure that the type of signature line used corresponds exactly with the person or business entity who is joining in the signing of a document.

The following notary acknowledgments and signature lines are intended to be used for the specific purposes outlined below. When preparing a legal document, choose the correct version of these additions carefully. The following are contained in this chapter:

Individual Acknowledgment: This clause should be used on documents where an individual is one of the parties who is to sign the document and the document needs to be notarized. However, if the document is to be signed by a wife and husband together, use the appropriate acknowledgment form explained below.

Individual Signature Line: This line should be inserted on all documents where a party that will sign the document is an individual. Again, however, if the document is to be signed by a wife and husband together, use the appropriate signature line which follows.

Wife and Husband Acknowledgment: This clause should be used on documents where both a wife and husband are to sign the document and the document needs to be notarized.

Wife and Husband Signature Line: This line should be inserted on all documents where both a wife and husband are intended to sign the document.

Power of Attorney Acknowledgment: This clause should be used on documents where an individual acting under a power of attorney is one of the parties who is to sign the document and the document needs to be notarized. As noted in Chapter 4: *Powers of Attorney*, an *attorney-in-fact* is a person who is authorized to act for another person by virtue of a document entitled a *Power of Attorney*, which will be further explained in the next chapter.

Power of Attorney Signature Line: This line should be inserted on all documents where a party that will sign the document is an individual acting under a power of attorney. The person signing must have the specific authority to act for another person under some form of Power of Attorney. The date of the Power of Attorney form should be noted.

Individual Acknowledgment

State of _____
County of _____

On _____ , 20 _____ , _____
personally came before me and, being duly sworn, did state that he or she is the
person described in the above document and that he or she signed the above document in my presence as a free and voluntary act for the purposes stated.

_____
Signature of Notary Public

Notary Public, In and for the County of _____
State of _____

My commission expires: _____   Notary Seal

Individual Signature Line

_____
Signature

_____
Printed Name

Wife and Husband Acknowledgment

State of _____
County of _____

On _____ , 20 _____ , _____
and _____ personally came before me and, being
duly sworn, did state that they are the wife and husband described in the above
document and that they signed the above document in my presence as a free and
voluntary act for the purposes stated.

_____
Signature of Notary Public

Notary Public, In and for the County of _____
State of _____

My commission expires: _____   Notary Seal

Wife and Husband Signature Line

_____   _____
Signature of Wife   Signature of Husband

_____   _____
Printed Name of Wife   Printed Name of Husband

Power of Attorney Acknowledgment

State of _____

County of _____

On _____ , 20 _____ , _____
personally came before me and, being duly sworn, did state that he or she is the
attorney-in-fact of _____ described in the above
document, that he or she signed the above document in my presence as attorney-
in-fact on behalf of this person, and that he or she had full authority to do so under
Power of Attorney dated _____ , 20 _____ .

_____
Signature of Notary Public

Notary Public, In and for the County of _____
State of _____

My commission expires: _____   Notary Seal

Power of Attorney Signature Line

_____
Signature of Person Holding Power of Attorney

_____
Printed Name of Person Holding Power of Attorney

As attorney-in-fact for _____

Under Power of Attorney dated _____ , 20 _____

CHAPTER 4
Powers of Attorney

A *power of attorney* form is a document that is used to allow one person to give the authority to act on his or her behalf to another person. The person signing the power of attorney grants legal authority to another person to "stand in his or her shoes" and act legally for him or her. The person who receives the power of attorney is called an *attorney-in-fact*. However, this title and the power of attorney form does not mean that the person receiving the power has to be a lawyer.

Power of attorney forms are useful documents for many occasions. They can be used to authorize someone else to sign certain documents if you cannot be present when the signatures are necessary. For example, a real estate closing in another state can be completed without your presence by providing a power of attorney to a real estate agent (or even a friend) that authorizes him or her to sign the documents on your behalf. Similarly, if you must be away from your home on a trip, and certain actions must be made in your absence, a power of attorney may be granted to enable another person to legally perform on your behalf. The form can also be used to allow your accountant to negotiate with the IRS, allow your secretary to sign checks and temporarily operate your business, or for many other purposes.

Traditionally, property matters were the type of actions handled with powers of attorney. Increasingly, however, people are using a specific type of power of attorney to authorize other persons to act on their behalf in the event of disability. This broad type of power of attorney is called a *durable power of attorney*. A durable power of attorney is intended to remain in effect even if a person becomes disabled or incompetent. All states have passed legislation that specifically authorizes this type of power of attorney. The durable power of attorney forms that are included in this book are intended to be used to allow another person to handle financial matters for an incapacitated person. The forms and the powers that these forms provide only go into effect upon the certification by one's primary physician that the person granting the power is incapacitated. Both the unlimited and limited durable power of attorney forms require notarization of the forms and the use of two witnesses to the signature, even though this in not a technical requirement in all states. The use of a notary public and witnesses will generally prevent delays or challenges to the powers that are granted in the durable power of attorney. Please note that these durable power of attorney forms are not intended to be used to make healthcare decisions on behalf of another person. The legal form that allows another person to make various healthcare decisions on behalf of an incapacitated person is referred to as a *durable power of attorney for healthcare*. This type of form is beyond the scope of this book and is not included. Please refer to Nova Publishing Company's *Living Wills Simplified*, by Dan Sitarz, for information on preparing this type of form. *Note*: Powers of attorney are very powerful legal documents. They can be used to grant virtually unlimited legal power to another person. You are advised to proceed with caution when using any of these forms. If you have any questions regarding their use, please consult a competent attorney.

Unlimited Power of Attorney: This form should be used only in situations where you desire to authorize another person to act for you in *all* transactions. The grant of power under this document is unlimited. However, please be advised that some states may require that you specifically spell out the authority granted to perform certain acts. Generally, however, for personal and property transactions, this broad grant of power will be effective. All that is necessary are the names and addresses of both the person granting the power and the person receiving the power. Both persons should sign the document. The signature of the person granting the power should be notarized and witnessed by two people.

Limited Power of Attorney: This document provides for a *limited* grant of authority to another person. It should be used in those situations when you need to authorize another person to act for you in a specific manner or to perform a specific action. The type of acts that you authorize the other person to perform should be spelled out in detail to avoid confusion (for example, to sign any necessary forms to complete the closing of the sale of real estate). What is needed to complete this form are the names and addresses of the person granting the power and the person receiving the power, and a full and detailed description of the powers granted. Both persons should sign the document. The signature of the person granting the power should be notarized and witnessed by two people.

Durable Unlimited Power of Attorney: Like the Unlimited Power of Attorney described above, this form should be used only in a situation in which you desire to authorize another person to act for you in *all* transactions. The grant of power under this document is unlimited. However, unlike the general Unlimited Power of Attorney, this form remains in effect *even* if you are incapacitated or disabled. This broad grant of power will be effective to allow your attorney-in-fact to perform on your behalf in the event of your disability. To complete this form, the name and address of the person granting the power and also of the person receiving the power should be filled in. Both persons should sign the document. The signature of the person granting the power should be notarized and witnessed by two other persons at the same time. The person receiving the power of attorney cannot be one of the witnesses.

Durable Limited Power of Attorney: Like the Limited Power of Attorney described above, this document provides for a *limited* grant of authority to another person. It should be used in those situations where you need to authorize another to act for you in a specific manner or to perform a specific action. However, this form remains in effect *even* if you are incapacitated or disabled. The limited grant of power provided by this document will be effective to allow your attorney-in-fact to perform on your behalf in the event of your disability. To complete this form, the names and addresses of both the person granting the power and the person receiving the power should be filled in. A full and detailed description of the powers granted should be inserted. Both persons should sign the document. The signature of the person granting the power should be notarized and witnessed by two other persons at the same time. The person receiving the power of attorney cannot be one of the witnesses.

Revocation of Power of Attorney: This document may be used with any of the above four power of attorney forms. The revocation is used to terminate the original authority that was granted to the other person in the first place. If the grant of power was for a limited purpose and that purpose is complete, this revocation should be used as soon after the transaction as possible. In any event, if you choose to revoke a power of attorney, a copy of this revocation should be provided to the person to whom the power was given. Copies should also be given to any party that may have had dealings with the attorney-in-fact before the revocation and to any party with whom the attorney-in-fact may be expected to attempt to deal with after the revocation.

Unlimited Power of Attorney

I, _____ ,
address:

grant an unlimited power of attorney to _____ ,
address:

to act as my attorney-in-fact.

I give my attorney-in-fact the maximum power under law to perform any act on my behalf that I could do personally, including but not limited to, all acts relating to any and all of my financial transactions and/or business affairs including all banking and financial institution transactions, all real estate or personal property transactions, all insurance or annuity transactions, all claims and litigation, and any and all business transactions. My attorney-in-fact is granted full power to act on my behalf in the same manner as if I were personally present. My attorney-in-fact accepts this appointment and agrees to act in my best interest as he or she considers advisable. This power of attorney may be revoked by me at any time and is automatically revoked upon my death or incapacitation. My attorney-in-fact shall not be compensated for his or her services nor shall my attorney-in-fact be liable to me, my estate, heirs, successors, or assigns for acting or refraining from acting under this document, except for willful misconduct or gross negligence. Any third party who receives a signed copy of this document may act under it. Revocation of this document is not effective unless a third party has actual knowledge of such revocation.

Dated _____ , 20 _____

_____
Signature of Person Granting Power of Attorney

_____
Printed Name of Person Granting Power of Attorney

_____

Signature of Witness #1

_____

Printed Name of Witness #1

State of _____

County of _____

On _____ , 20 _____ , _____ personally
came before me and, being duly sworn, did state that he or she is the person described in the
above document and that he or she signed the above document in my presence.

_____

Signature of Notary Public

Notary Public, In and for the County of _____
State of _____

My commission expires: _____   Notary Seal

I accept my appointment as attorney-in-fact.

_____

Signature of Person Granted Power of Attorney

_____

Printed Name of Person Granted Power of Attorney

_____

Signature of Witness #2

_____

Printed Name of Witness #2

Limited Power of Attorney

I, _____ ,
address:

grant a limited power of attorney to _____ ,
address:

to act as my attorney-in-fact.

I give my attorney-in-fact the maximum power under law to perform the following specific acts on my behalf:

My attorney-in-fact accepts this appointment and agrees to act in my best interest as he or she considers advisable. This power of attorney may be revoked by me at any time and is automatically revoked upon my death or incapacitation. My attorney-in-fact shall not be compensated for his or her services nor shall my attorney-in-fact be liable to me, my estate, heirs, successors, or assigns for acting or refraining from acting under this document, except for willful misconduct or gross negligence. Any third party who receives a signed copy of this document may act under it. Revocation of this document is not effective unless a third party has actual knowledge of such revocation.

Dated _____ , 20 _____

_____
Signature of Person Granting Power of Attorney

_____
Printed Name of Person Granting Power of Attorney

_____   _____
Signature of Witness #1   Signature of Witness #2

_____   _____
Printed Name of Witness #1   Printed Name of Witness #2

State of _____
County of _____

On _____ , 20 _____ , _____ personally
came before me and, being duly sworn, did state that he or she is the person described in the
above document and that he or she signed the above document in my presence.

_____
Signature of Notary Public

Notary Public, In and for the County of _____
State of _____

My commission expires: _____   Notary Seal

I accept my appointment as attorney-in-fact.

_____
Signature of Person Granted Power of Attorney

_____
Printed Name of Person Granted Power of Attorney

Durable Unlimited Power of Attorney

I, _____ ,
address:

grant an unlimited durable power of attorney to _____ ,
address:

to act as my attorney-in-fact.

This power of attorney shall become effective upon my incapacitation, as certified by my primary physician, or if my primary physician is not available, by any other attending physician. This power of attorney grants no power or authority regarding healthcare decisions to my designated attorney-in-fact. I give my attorney-in-fact the maximum power under law to perform any act on my behalf that I could do personally, including but not limited to, all acts relating to any and all of my financial transactions and/or business affairs including all banking and financial institution transactions, all real estate or personal property transactions, all insurance or annuity transactions, all claims and litigation, and any and all business transactions. My attorney-in-fact is granted full power to act on my behalf in the same manner as if I were personally present. My attorney-in-fact accepts this appointment and agrees to act in my best interest as he or she considers advisable. This power of attorney may be revoked by me at any time and is automatically revoked upon my death. This power of attorney shall not be affected by my present or future disability or incapacity. My attorney-in-fact shall not be compensated for his or her services nor shall my attorney-in-fact be liable to me, my estate, heirs, successors, or assigns for acting or refraining from acting under this document, except for willful misconduct or gross negligence. Any third party who receives a signed copy of this document may act under it. Revocation of this document is not effective unless a third party has actual knowledge of such revocation.

Dated _____ , 20 _____

_____
Signature of Person Granting Power of Attorney

_____
Printed Name of Person Granting Power of Attorney

_____   _____
Signature of Witness #1   Signature of Witness #2

_____   _____
Printed Name of Witness #1   Printed Name of Witness #2

State of _____
County of _____

On _____, 20 _____, _____ personally
came before me and, being duly sworn, did state that he or she is the person described in the
above document and that he or she signed the above document in my presence.

_____
Signature of Notary Public

Notary Public, In and for the County of _____
State of _____

My commission expires: _____   Notary Seal

I accept my appointment as attorney-in-fact.

_____
Signature of Person Granted Power of Attorney

_____
Printed Name of Person Granted Power of Attorney

Durable Limited Power of Attorney

I, _____ ,
address:

grant a limited durable power of attorney to _____ ,
address:

to act as my attorney-in-fact.

I give my attorney-in-fact the maximum power under law to perform the following specific acts on my behalf:

This power of attorney shall become effective upon my incapacitation, as certified by my primary physician, or if my primary physician is not available, by any other attending physician. This power of attorney grants no power or authority regarding healthcare decisions to my designated attorney-in-fact. My attorney-in-fact accepts this appointment and agrees to act in my best interest as he or she considers advisable. This power of attorney may be revoked by me at any time and is automatically revoked upon my death. This power of attorney shall not be affected by my present or future disability or incapacity. My attorney-in-fact shall not be compensated for his or her services nor shall my attorney-in-fact be liable to me, my estate, heirs, successors, or assigns for acting or refraining from acting under this document, except for willful misconduct or gross negligence. Any third party who receives a signed copy of this document may act under it. Revocation of this document is not effective unless a third party has actual knowledge of such revocation.

Dated _____ , 20 _____

_____
Signature of Person Granting Power of Attorney

_____
Printed Name of Person Granting Power of Attorney

_____ _____
Signature of Witness #1   Signature of Witness #2

_____ _____
Printed Name of Witness #1   Printed Name of Witness #2

State of _____
County of _____

On _____ , 20 _____ , _____ personally
came before me and, being duly sworn, did state that he or she is the person described in the
above document and that he or she signed the above document in my presence.

_____
Signature of Notary Public

Notary Public, In and for the County of _____
State of _____

My commission expires: _____   Notary Seal

I accept my appointment as attorney-in-fact.

_____
Signature of Person Granted Power of Attorney

_____
Printed Name of Person Granted Power of Attorney

Revocation of Power of Attorney

I, _____ ,
address:

revoke the power of attorney dated _____ ,
which was granted to _____ ,
address:

to act as my attorney-in-fact.

Dated _____ , 20 _____

_____
Signature of Person Revoking Power of Attorney

_____
Printed Name of Person Revoking Power of Attorney

State of _____
County of _____

On _____ , 20 _____ , _____ personally
came before me and, being duly sworn, did state that he or she is the person described in the
above document and that he or she signed the above document in my presence.

_____
Signature of Notary Public

Notary Public, In and for the County of _____
State of _____

My commission expires: _____   Notary Seal

CHAPTER 5
Wills

A *will* is a legal document that, when accepted by a probate court, is proof of an intent to transfer property to the persons or organizations named in the will upon the death of the maker of the will. The maker of the will is known as the *testator*. A will is effective for the transfer of property that is owned by the testator upon his or her death. A will can be changed, modified, or revoked at any time by the testator prior to his or her death.

It is equally important to understand that in order for a will to be valid, it must generally be prepared, witnessed, and signed according to certain technical legal procedures. Although a will is perfectly valid if it is written in plain English and does not use technical legal language, it *must* be prepared, witnessed, and signed in the manner outlined in this book. This cannot be overemphasized. You cannot take any shortcuts when following the instructions as they relate to the procedures necessary for completing and signing your will. These procedures are not at all difficult and consist generally of carefully preparing your will in the manner outlined later in this chapter, signing it in the manner specified, and having three witnesses and a notary public also sign the document. (Although not a legal requirement, the notarization of your will can aid in its proof of existence in court later, if necessary). *Note:* Wills in this book are not valid for Louisiana residents. Please consult Nova Publishing Company's *Basic Wills Simplified*, by Daniel Sitarz, or contact a competent attorney.

Note: In some cases (for example, those involving extremely complicated business or personal financial holdings, those that involve the desire to create a complex trust arrangement, or if you are unsure of the correct use of any of the forms in this chapter), it is clearly advisable to consult an attorney for the preparation of your will. However, in most circumstances and for most people, the terms of a will that will provide for the necessary protection are relatively routine and may be safely prepared without the added expense of consulting a lawyer.

Before you begin to actually prepare your own will, you must understand what your assets are, who your beneficiaries are to be, and what your personal desires are as to how those assets should be distributed among your beneficiaries. The following Property and Beneficiary Questionnaires will assist you in that task. When you have finished completing these questionnaires, have them before you as you select and prepare your personal will.

Property Questionnaire Instructions

In general, by using a will, you can bequeath any property that you own at the time of your death. However, there are forms of property that you may "own," but which may not be transferred by way of a will. In addition, you may own only a percentage or share of certain other property. In such situations, only that percentage or share that you actually own may be left by your will. Finally, there are types of property ownership that are automatically transferred to another party at your death, regardless of the presence of a will.

In the first category of property that *cannot* be transferred by will are properties that have a designated beneficiary outside of the provisions of your will. In general, if there is already a valid determination of who will receive the property upon your death (as there is, for example, in the choice of a life insurance beneficiary), you may not alter this choice of beneficiary through the use of your will. If you wish to alter your choice of beneficiary in any of these cases, please alter the choice directly with the holder of the particular property (for instance, the life insurance company or bank). These types of properties include:

- Life insurance policies
- Retirement plans
- IRAs and KEOGHs
- Pension plans
- Trust bank accounts
- Living trust assets
- Payable-on-death bank accounts
- U.S. Savings Bonds, with payable-on-death beneficiaries

The next category of property that may have certain restrictions regarding its transfer by will is property of which you may own only a certain share or percentage. Examples of this may be a partnership interest in a company or a jointly-held property. Using a will, you may leave only that percentage or fraction of the ownership of the property that is actually yours.

The ownership rights and shares of property owned jointly must be considered. Several states, mostly in the western United States, follow the *community property* type of marital property system. The community property states are: Alaska, Arizona, California, Idaho, Louisiana, Nevada, New Mexico, Texas, Washington, and Wisconsin. All property owned by either spouse during a marriage is divided into two types: separate property and community property. *Separate property* consists of all property considered to be owned entirely by one spouse. Separate property, essentially, is all property owned by the spouse prior to the marriage and kept separate during the marriage, and all property received individually by the spouse by gift or inheritance during the marriage. All other property is considered *community property*. In other words, all property acquired during the marriage by either spouse, unless by gift or inheritance, is community property. Community property is considered to be owned in equal shares by each spouse, regardless of whose efforts actually went into acquiring the property. *Note*: Alaska allows spouses to create community property by mutual agreement. (One major exception to this general rule are Social Security and railroad retirement benefits, which are considered to be separate property by Federal law). Thus, if you are a married resident of a community property state, the property that you may dispose of by will consists of all of your separate property and one-half of your jointly owned marital community property. The other half of the community property automatically becomes your spouse's sole property upon your death. Residents of community property states may also own property jointly as *tenants-in-common* or as *joint tenants* (for an explanation of these terms, please refer to the Glossary on the enclosed Forms-on-CD).

Residents of all other states are governed by a *common-law property* system. Under this system, there is no rule that gives 50 percent ownership of the property acquired during marriage to each spouse. In common-law states, the property that you may dispose of with your will consists of all the property held by title in your name, any property that you have earned or purchased with your own money, and any property that you may have been given as a gift or inherited, either before or after your marriage.

If your name alone is on a title document (for instance, a deed or automobile title) in common-law states, then you own it solely. If your name and your spouse's name are both on the document, you generally own it as tenants-in-common, unless the document specifically states that your ownership is to be as joint tenants or, if your state allows, as a *tenancy-by-the-entireties* (a form of joint tenancy between married persons). There is an important difference between these types of joint ownership: namely, survivorship. With property owned as tenants-in-common, the percentage or fraction that each tenant-in-common owns is property that may be disposed of under a will. If the property is held as joint tenants or as tenants-by-the entireties, the survivor automatically receives the deceased party's share. Thus, in your will, you may not dispose of any property held in joint tenancy or tenancy-by-the entirety since it already has an automatic legal disposition upon your death. If you are married however, there is a further restriction on your right to dispose of property by will. All common-law states protect spouses from total disinheritance by providing a statutory scheme under which a spouse may choose to take a minimum share of the deceased spouse's estate, regardless of what the will states. This effectively prevents any spouse from being entirely disinherited through the use of the common-law rules of property (in other words, name on the title = ownership of the property).

Use the following Property Questionnaire to determine your assets, liabilities, and net worth.

Property Questionnaire

What Are Your Assets?

Cash and Bank Accounts

Individual accounts can be left by will; joint tenancy and payable-on-death accounts cannot.

Checking Account .... $ _____
Bank _____
Account number _____
Name(s) on account _____

Savings Account .... $ _____
Bank _____
Account number _____
Name(s) on account _____

Certificate of Deposit .... $ _____
Held by _____
Expiration date _____
Name(s) on account _____

Other Account .... $ _____
Bank _____
Account number _____
Name(s) on account _____

Total Cash and Bank Accounts .... (A) $ _____

Life Insurance and Annuity Contracts

Life insurance benefits cannot be left by will.

Ordinary Life .... $ _____
Company _____
Policy number _____
Beneficiary _____
Address _____

Endowment .... $ _____
Company _____
Policy number _____
Beneficiary _____
Address _____

Term Life .... $ _____
Company _____
Policy number _____
Beneficiary _____
Address _____

Annuity Contract .... $ _____
Company _____
Policy number _____
Beneficiary _____
Address _____

Total Life Insurance and Annuity Contracts .... (B) $ _____

Accounts and Notes Receivable

Debts payable to you may be left by will.

Accounts Receivable .... $ _____
Due from _____
Address _____

Notes Receivable .... $ _____
Due from _____
Address _____

Other Debts .... $ _____
Due from _____
Address _____

Other Debts .... $ _____
Due from _____
Address _____

Total Accounts and Notes Receivable .... (C) $ _____

Stocks and Mutual Funds

Ownership of individually-held stock and mutual funds may be left by will.

Company _____

CUSIP or certificate number _____

Number and type of shares _____

Value .... $ _____

Company _____

CUSIP or certificate number _____

Number and type of shares _____

Value .... $ _____

Total Stocks and Mutual Funds .... (D) $ _____

Bonds and Mutual Bond Funds

Ownership of individually-held bonds and mutual bond funds may be left by will.

Company _____

CUSIP or certificate number _____

Number and type of shares _____

Value .... $ _____

Company _____

CUSIP or certificate number _____

Number and type of shares _____

Value .... $ _____

Total Bonds and Mutual Bond Funds .... (E) $ _____

Business Interests

Ownership of business interests may generally be left by will.

Individual Proprietorship

Name _____

Location _____

Type of business _____

Your net value .... $ _____

46

Interest in Partnership
Name _____
Location _____
Type of business _____
Gross value .... $ _____
Percentage interest   _____ %
Your net value .... $ _____

Closely-held Corporation Interest
Name _____
Location _____
Type of business _____
Gross value .... $ _____
Percentage of shares held   _____ %
Your net value .... $ _____

Total Business Interests .... (F) $ _____

Real Estate

Property owned individually or as tenants-in-common may be left by will. Property held in joint tenancy or tenancy-by-the-entirety may not.

Personal Residence
Location _____
Value .... $ _____
How is property held (joint tenants, tenancy-in-common, etc.)? _____
What is your percent?   _____ %
Value of your share .... $ _____

Vacation Home
Location _____
Value .... $ _____
How is property held (joint tenants, tenancy-in-common, etc.)? _____
What is your percent?   _____ %
Value of your share .... $ _____

Vacant Land
Location _____
Value .... $ _____
How is property held (joint tenants, tenancy-in-common, etc.)? _____
What is your percent?   _____ %
Value of your share .... $ _____

Income Property
Location _____
Value .... $ _____
How is property held (joint tenants, tenancy-in-common, etc.)? _____
What is your percent?   _____ %
Value of your share .... $ _____

Other Property
Location _____
Value .... $ _____
How is property held (joint tenants, tenancy-in-common, etc.)? _____
What is your percent?   _____ %
Value of your share .... $ _____

Total Real Estate .... (G) $ _____

Personal Property

Personal property owned individually or as a tenant-in-common may be left by will.

Car .... $ _____
Description _____

Car .... $ _____
Description _____

Other Vehicle .... $ _____
Description _____

Furniture .... $ _____
Description _____

Furniture .... $ _____
Description _____

Appliance .... $ _____
Description _____

Jewelry and Furs .... $ _____
Description _____

Music System .... $ _____
Description _____

48

Artwork .... $ _____
Description _____

Other .... $ _____
Description _____

Other .... $ _____
Description _____

Total Personal Property .... (H) $ _____

Miscellaneous Assets

Royalties .... $ _____
Description _____

Patents .... $ _____
Description _____

Copyrights .... $ _____
Description _____

Heirlooms .... $ _____
Description _____

Heirlooms .... $ _____
Description _____

Heirlooms .... $ _____
Description _____

Other .... $ _____
Description _____

Other .... $ _____
Description _____

Other .... $ _____
Description _____

Total Miscellaneous Assets .... (I) $ _____

Employee Benefit and Pension/Profit-Sharing Plans

Retirement benefits cannot be left by will.

Company _____
Plan type _____
Net value .... $ _____

Company _____
Plan type _____
Net value .... $ _____

Total Employee Benefit and Pension/Profit-Sharing Plans .... (J) $ _____

Total Assets

Insert totals from previous pages.

Cash and Bank Accounts Total .... (A) $ _____
Life Insurance and Annuity Contracts Total .... (B) $ _____
Accounts and Notes Receivable Total .... (C) $ _____
Stocks and Mutual Funds Total .... (D) $ _____
Bonds and Mutual Fund Bonds Total .... (E) $ _____
Business Interests Total .... (F) $ _____
Real Estate Total .... (G) $ _____
Personal Property Total .... (H) $ _____
Miscellaneous Assets Total .... (I) $ _____
Employee Benefit and Pension/Profit-Sharing Plans Total .... (J) $ _____

Total Assets .... (1) $ _____

What Are Your Liabilities?

Notes and Loans Payable

Payable to _____
Address _____
Term _____
Interest rate _____ %
Amount due .... $ _____

Payable to _____
Address _____
Term _____
Interest rate _____ %
Amount due .... $ _____

Total Notes and Loans Payable .... (K) $ _____

Accounts Payable

Payable to _____
Address _____
Term _____
Interest rate _____ %
Amount due .... $ _____

Payable to _____
Address _____
Term _____
Interest rate _____ %
Amount due .... $ _____

Total Accounts Payable .... (L) $ _____

Mortgages Payable

Property Location _____
Payable to _____
Address _____
Term _____
Interest rate _____ %
Amount due .... $ _____

Property Location _____

Payable to _____

Address _____

Term _____

Interest rate   _____ %

Amount due .... $ _____

Total Mortgages Payable .... (M) $ _____

Taxes Payable

Federal Income Taxes .... $ _____

State Income Taxes .... $ _____

Personal Property Taxes .... $ _____

Real Estate Taxes .... $ _____

Payroll Taxes .... $ _____

Other Taxes .... $ _____

Other Taxes .... $ _____

Other Taxes .... $ _____

Total Taxes Payable .... (N) $ _____

Credit Card Accounts Payable

Credit Card Company _____

Credit card account number _____

Address _____

Interest rate   _____ %

Amount due .... $ _____

Credit Card Company _____

Credit card account number _____

Address _____

Interest rate   _____ %

Amount due .... $ _____

Credit Card Company _____

Credit card account number _____

Address _____

Interest rate   _____ %

Amount due .... $ _____

Total Credit Card Accounts Payable .... (O) $ _____

52

Miscellaneous Liabilities Payable

To Whom Due _____

Address _____

Term _____

Interest rate _____ %

Amount due .... $ _____

To Whom Due _____

Address _____

Term _____

Interest rate _____ %

Amount due .... $ _____

Total Miscellaneous Liabilities Payable .... (P) $ _____

Total Liabilities

Insert totals from previous pages.

Notes and Loans Payable Total .... (K) $ _____

Accounts Payable Total .... (L) $ _____

Mortgages Payable Total .... (M) $ _____

Taxes Payable Total .... (N) $ _____

Credit Card Accounts Payable Total .... (O) $ _____

Miscellaneous Liabilities Payable Total .... (P) $ _____

Total Liabilities .... (2) $ _____

Net Worth of Your Estate

Total Assets .... (1) $ _____

Minus (-) *Total Liabilities* .... (2) $ _____

Equals (=) **Your Total Net Worth** .... $ _____

Beneficiary Questionnaire Instructions

Any person or organization who receives property under a will is termed a *beneficiary* of that will. Any person or organization can receive property under a will unless the beneficiary falls into certain narrow categories of disqualification. Those who can receive property as beneficiaries include any family members, the named executor, any illegitimate children (if named specifically), corporations, charities (but see below for possible restrictions), creditors, debtors, and any friends, acquaintances, or even strangers. The few categories of disqualified beneficiaries are as follows:

- An attorney who drafts the will is generally assumed to have used undue influence if he or she is made a beneficiary

- Many states disqualify any witnesses to the execution of the will. However, to be safe, it is recommended that none of your witnesses be beneficiaries under your will

- A person who murders someone is universally disqualified from receiving any property under the murdered person's will

- An unincorporated association is typically not allowed to receive property under a will. This particular disqualification stems from the fact that such associations generally have no legal right to hold property

- A few states also have restrictions on the right to leave property to charitable organizations and churches. If you intend to leave large sums of money or property to a charitable organization or church, please check with a competent attorney or consult Nova Publishing Company's *Prepare Your Own Will: The National Will Kit*, or *Basic Wills Simplified*, both by Daniel Sitarz, for further information on state-by-state restrictions

You are advised to review your will periodically and make any necessary changes as your marital or family situation may dictate. If you are divorced, married, remarried, widowed, or adopt or have a child, there may be unforeseen consequences based on the way you have written your will. Each state has differing laws on the effect of marriage and divorce on a person's will. Your will should be prepared with regard to how your life is presently arranged. Your will should, however, always be reviewed and updated each time there is a substantial change in your life.

Beneficiary Questionnaire

Who Will Receive Which of Your Assets?

Spouse

Spouse _____

    Maiden name _____

    Date of marriage _____

    Date of birth _____

    Address _____

    Current income .... $ _____

    Amount, specific items, or share of estate that you desire to leave _____

    _____

    Alternate beneficiary _____

Children

Child _____

    Date of birth _____

    Address _____

    Spouse's name (if any) _____

    Amount, specific items, or share of estate that you desire to leave _____

    _____

    Alternate beneficiary _____

Child _____

    Date of birth _____

    Address _____

    Spouse's name (if any) _____

    Amount, specific items, or share of estate that you desire to leave _____

    _____

    Alternate beneficiary _____

Child _____
    Date of birth _____
    Address _____

    _____
    Spouse's name (if any) _____
    Amount, specific items, or share of estate that you desire to leave _____

    _____
    _____
    Alternate beneficiary _____

Grandchildren

Grandchild _____
    Date of birth _____
    Address _____

    _____
    Spouse's name (if any) _____
    Amount, specific items, or share of estate that you desire to leave _____

    _____
    _____
    Alternate beneficiary _____

Grandchild _____
    Date of birth _____
    Address _____

    _____
    Spouse's name (if any) _____
    Amount, specific items, or share of estate that you desire to leave _____

    _____
    _____
    Alternate beneficiary _____

Grandchild _____
    Date of birth _____
    Address _____

    _____
    Spouse's name (if any) _____
    Amount, specific items, or share of estate that you desire to leave _____

    _____
    _____
    Alternate beneficiary _____

Parents

Parent _____
    Date of birth _____
    Address _____
    _____
    Spouse's name (if any) _____
    Amount, specific items, or share of estate that you desire to leave _____
    _____
    _____
    Alternate beneficiary _____

Parent _____
    Date of birth _____
    Address _____
    _____
    Spouse's name (if any) _____
    Amount, specific items, or share of estate that you desire to leave _____
    _____
    _____
    Alternate beneficiary _____

Siblings

Sibling _____
    Date of birth _____
    Address _____
    _____
    Spouse's name (if any) _____
    Amount, specific items, or share of estate that you desire to leave _____
    _____
    _____
    Alternate beneficiary _____

Sibling _____
    Date of birth _____
    Address _____
    _____
    Spouse's name (if any) _____
    Amount, specific items, or share of estate that you desire to leave _____
    _____
    _____
    Alternate beneficiary _____

Other Dependents

Other Dependent _____

    Date of birth _____

    Address _____

_____

    Spouse's name (if any) _____

    Amount, specific items, or share of estate that you desire to leave _____

_____

_____

    Alternate beneficiary _____

Other Dependent _____

    Date of birth _____

    Address _____

_____

    Spouse's name (if any) _____

    Amount, specific items, or share of estate that you desire to leave _____

_____

_____

    Alternate beneficiary _____

Are There Any Other Relatives, Friends, or Organizations to Whom You Wish to Leave Gifts?

Name _____

    Relationship _____

    Address _____

_____

    Spouse's name (if any) _____

    Amount, specific items, or share of estate that you desire to leave _____

_____

_____

    Alternate beneficiary _____

Name _____

    Relationship _____

    Address _____

_____

    Spouse's name (if any) _____

    Amount, specific items, or share of estate that you desire to leave _____

_____

_____

    Alternate beneficiary _____

Name _____
    Relationship _____
    Address _____

    _____
    Spouse's name (if any) _____
    Amount, specific items, or share of estate that you desire to leave _____

    _____

    Alternate beneficiary _____

Are There Any Persons Whom You Wish to Specifically Leave out of Your Will?

Name _____
    Relationship _____
    Address _____

    _____
    Spouse's name (if any) _____
    Reason for disinheritance _____

    _____

    _____

Name _____
    Relationship _____
    Address _____

    _____
    Spouse's name (if any) _____
    Reason for disinheritance _____

    _____

    _____

Name _____
    Relationship _____

    Address _____

    _____
    Spouse's name (if any) _____
    Reason for disinheritance _____

    _____

    _____

Preparing Your Will

In this section are contained four separate wills that have been prepared for the purpose of allowing persons whose situations fall into certain standard formats to prepare their wills quickly and easily on pre-assembled forms. Generally, the wills are for a single person with or without children and for a married person with or without children. Please read the description prior to each will to be certain that the will you choose is appropriate for your particular situation. Also note that each of the wills in this book is intended to be a *self-proving* will. This means that the signatures of the witnesses and the testator will be verified by a notary public and thus, the witnesses' testimony will not be needed in probate court at a later date in order to authenticate their signatures.

Instructions

These pre-assembled will forms are intended to be used as simplified worksheets for preparing your own personal will. The forms should be filled-in by hand and then retyped according to the instructions, or prepared using the Forms-on-CD, as explained on the CD's "readme.doc" file. These pre-assembled wills are not intended to be filled in and used "as is" as an original will. Such use would most likely result in an invalid will. Be certain to carefully follow all of the instructions for use of these forms. The forms are not difficult to fill out, but must be prepared properly in order to be legally valid. To prepare any of the wills in this chapter, you should follow these simple steps:

1. Carefully read through all of the clauses in the blank pre-assembled will form to determine if the clauses provided are suitable for your situation. Choose the will that is most appropriate. Make a photocopy of the will that you select to use as a worksheet. If you wish, you may use the form in the book itself as a worksheet (unless it is a library book!)

2. Using your Property and Beneficiary Questionnaires, fill in the appropriate information where necessary on these forms.

3. After you have filled in all of the appropriate information, carefully reread your entire will. Be certain that it contains all of the correct information that you desire. Then, starting at the beginning of the will, cross out all of the words and phrases in the pre-assembled will form that do not apply in your situation.

4. When you have completed all of your will clauses, turn to page 94 for instructions on the typing and final preparation of your will.

As you fill in the information for each clause, keep in mind the following instructions:

Title Clause: The title clause is mandatory for all wills and must be included. Fill in the name blank with your full legal name. If you have been known by more than one name, use your principal name.

Identification Clause: The identification clause is mandatory and must be included in all wills. In the first blank, include any other names that you are known by. Do this by adding the phrase: "also known as" after your principal full name. For example:

> John James Smith, also known as Jimmy John Smith.

In the spaces provided for your residence, use the location of your principal residence; that is, the place where you currently live permanently.

Marital Status Clause: Each of the pre-assembled will forms in this chapter is either for a married or single person. Select the proper will and if you are married, fill in the appropriate information. If you have previously been married, please add and complete the following sentence:

> I was previously married to [_name of your former spouse_], and that marriage ended by [_select either death, divorce, or annulment_].

Identification of Children Clause: This clause will only be present in the pre-assembled wills that relate to children. In this clause, you should specifically identify all of your children, indicating their full names, current addresses, and dates of birth. Cross out those spaces that are not used.

Identification of Grandchildren Clause: This clause will only be used in the pre-assembled wills that relate to grandchildren. If you do not have grandchildren, cross out this entire clause. If you do have grandchildren, you should specifically identify all of your grandchildren in this clause, indicating their full names, current addresses, and dates of birth. Cross out those spaces that are not used.

Specific Gifts Clause: For making specific gifts, use as many of the "I give ..." paragraphs as is necessary to complete your chosen gifts. In these paragraphs, you may make any type of gift that you wish; either a cash gift, a gift of a specific piece of personal property or real estate, or a specific share of your total estate. If you wish to give some of your estate in the form of portions of the total, it is recommended to use fractional portions. For example, if you wish to leave your estate in equal shares to two persons, use "I give one-half of my total estate to…" for each party. Although none of the wills in this chapter contain a specific clause that states that you give one person your entire estate, you may make such a gift using this clause by simply stating:

> "I give my entire estate to…."

Be sure that you do not attempt to give any other gifts. However, you should still include the *residuary clause* in your will, which is explained below.

In your description of the property, you should be as specific and precise as possible. For land, it is suggested that you use the description exactly as shown on the deed to the property. For personal property, be certain that your description clearly differentiates your gift from any other property. For example: "I give my blue velvet coat which was a gift from my brother John to…." Use serial numbers, colors, or any other descriptive words to clearly indicate the exact nature of the gift. For cash gifts, specifically indicate the amount of the gift. For gifts of securities, state the amount of shares and the name of the company. You may add simple conditions to the gifts that you make, if you desire. For example, you may state "I give $1,000.00 to the Centerville Church for use in purchasing a new roof for the church." Complex conditions, however, are not possible in this clause, and immoral or illegal conditions are not acceptable.

Be sure to clearly identify the beneficiary and alternate beneficiary by their full names. You can also name joint beneficiaries, such as several children, if you choose. The space provided for an identification of the relationship of the beneficiary can simply be a descriptive phrase like "my wife," "my brother-in-law," or "my best friend." It does not mean that the beneficiary must be related to you personally.

The choice of alternate beneficiary is for the purpose of allowing you to designate someone else to receive the gift if your first choice to receive the gift dies before you do (or, in the case of a organization chosen as primary beneficiary, is no longer in business). In this or any of the other gift clauses, your choice for alternate beneficiary may be one or more persons or an organization. It is recommended to always specifically name your beneficiary(ies), rather than using a description only, such as "my children." In addition, you may delete the alternate beneficiary choice and substitute the words "the residue" instead. The *residue* is all property remaining in your estate after all expenses, taxes, and gifts have been paid. The result of this change will be that if your primary beneficiary dies before you do, your gift will pass under your residuary clause, which is discussed below. If additional gifts are desired, simply photocopy an additional page to use as a worksheet.

Residuary Clause: Although not a technical legal requirement, it is strongly recommended that you include the residuary clause in every will. With this clause, you will choose the person(s) or organization(s) to receive anything that is not covered by other clauses of your will. If, for any reason, any other gifts under your will are not able to be completed, this clause goes into effect. For example, if a beneficiary refuses to accept your gift, the chosen beneficiary has died and no alternate was selected, or both the beneficiary and alternate has died, the gift is put back into your estate and would *pass under* (be distributed under the terms of) the residuary clause. If there is no residuary clause included in your will, any property not disposed of under your will is treated as though you did not have a will and could potentially be forfeited to the state. To avoid this, it is strongly recommended that you make this clause mandatory in your will.

In addition, you may use this clause to give all of your estate (except your specific gifts) to one or more persons. For example: you make specific gifts of $1,000.00 to a sister and a car to a friend. By then naming your spouse as the residuary clause beneficiary, you will have gifted everything in your estate to your spouse—except the $1,000.00 and the car. You could then name your children, in equal shares, as the alternate residuary beneficiaries. In this manner, if your spouse were to die first, your children would then equally share your entire estate—except the $1,000.00 and the car.

Be sure to clearly identify the beneficiary by full name. The space provided for an identification of the relationship of the beneficiary can simply be a descriptive phrase like "my wife," "my brother-in-law," or "my best friend." It does not mean that the beneficiary must be related to you personally.

Survivorship Clause: This clause is included in every will. This clause provides for two possibilities. First, it provides for a required period of survival for any beneficiary, in order to receive a gift under your will. The practical effect of this is to be certain that your property passes under your will and not under that of a beneficiary who dies shortly after receiving your gift. The second portion of this clause provides for a determination of how your property should pass in the eventuality that both you and a beneficiary (most likely your spouse) should die in a manner that makes it impossible to determine who died first. Without this clause in your will, it would be possible that property could momentarily pass to a beneficiary under your will. When that person dies (possibly immediately, if a result of a common accident or disaster), your property could wind up being left to the person whom your beneficiary designated, rather than to your alternate beneficiary.

If you and your spouse are both preparing wills, it is a good idea to be certain that each of your wills contains identical survivorship clauses. If you are each other's primary beneficiary, it is also wise to attempt to coordinate who your alternate beneficiaries may be in the event of simultaneous deaths of you and your spouse.

Executor Clause: The executor clause must be included in every will. With this clause, you will make your choice of *executor*, the person who will administer and distribute your estate, and an alternate choice if your first choice is unable to serve. A spouse, sibling, or other trusted party is usually chosen to act as executor. The person chosen should be a resident of the state in which you currently reside.

Note that you allow your executor to seek independent administration of your estate. Where allowed by state law, this enables your executor to manage your estate with minimal court supervision and can save your estate extensive court costs and legal fees. Additionally, you grant the executor broad powers to manage your estate and also provide that he or she not be required to post a bond in order to be appointed to serve as executor.

Be sure to clearly identify the executor and alternate executor by their full names. The space provided for an identification of the relationship of the executor can simply be a descriptive phrase like "my wife," "my brother-in-law," or "my best friend." It does not mean that the executor must be related to you personally.

Child Guardianship Clause: This clause will only be present in the pre-assembled wills that relate to children. With this clause, you may designate your choice as to whom you wish to care for any of your minor children after you are gone. If none of your children are minors, you may delete this clause. Who you choose to be the guardian of your children is an important matter. If you are married, your spouse is generally appointed by the probate or family court, regardless of your designation in a will. However, even if you are married, it is a good idea to choose your spouse as first choice and then provide a second choice. This will cover the contingency in which both you and your spouse die in a single accident.

Your choice should obviously be a trusted person whom you feel would provide the best care for your children in your absence. Be aware, however, that the court is guided, but not bound, by this particular choice in your will. The court's decision in appointing a child's guardian is based upon what would be in the best interests of the child. In most situations, however, a parent's choice as to who should be his or her child's guardian is almost universally followed by the courts. Additionally, you grant the guardian broad power to care for and manage your children's property and also provide that the appointed guardian not be required to post a bond in order to be appointed.

Be sure to clearly identify the guardian and alternate guardian by full name. The space provided for an identification of the relationship of the guardian can simply be a descriptive phrase like "my wife," "my brother-in-law," or "my best friend." It does not mean that the guardian must be related to you personally.

Children's Trust Fund Clause: This clause will only be present in the pre-assembled wills that relate to children. It is by using this clause that you may set up a trust fund for any gifts you have made to your minor children. You also may delay the time when they will actually have unrestricted control over your gift. It is not recommended, however, to attempt to delay receipt of control beyond the age of 30. If you have left assets to more than one child, this clause provides that individual trusts be set up for each child. If none of your children are minors, you may delete this clause.

The choice for trustee under a children's trust should generally be the same person whom you have chosen to be the children's guardian. This is not, however, a requirement. The choice of trustee is generally a spouse if alive, with the alternate being a trusted friend or family member. Be sure to clearly identify the trustee and alternate trustee by full name. The space provided for an identification of the relationship of the trustee can simply be a descriptive phrase like "my wife," "my brother-in-law," or "my best friend." It does not mean that the trustee must be related to you personally.

The terms of the trust provide that the trustee may distribute any or all of the income or principal to the children as the trustee deems necessary to provide for the children's health, support, and education. The trust will terminate when either the child's specific age is reached, all of the money is spent prior to that age, or the child dies prematurely. Upon termination, any remaining trust funds will be distributed to the child (beneficiary) if surviving; if not surviving, to the heirs of the beneficiary (if any); or if there are no heirs of the beneficiary, to the residue of your estate. Additionally, you grant the trustee broad power to manage the trust and also provide that he or she not be required to post a bond in order to be appointed.

Organ Donation Clause: The use of this clause is optional. If you choose not to use this clause, you may delete it from your will. Use this clause to provide for any use of your body after death. You may, if you so desire, limit your donation to certain parts; for example, only your eyes. If so desired, simply delete "any of my body parts and/or organs" from the following provision and insert your chosen donation. A copy of your will or instructions regarding this donation should be kept in a place that is readily accessible by your executor and spouse.

Funeral Arrangements Clause: The use of this clause is optional. If you choose not to use this clause, you may delete it from your will. Use this clause to make known your wishes as to funeral and burial arrangements. Since it may be difficult to obtain your will quickly in an emergency, it is also a good idea to leave information regarding these desires with your executor, your spouse, a close friend, or a relative.

Signature and Self-Proving Clause: The signature lines and final paragraph of this clause must be included in your will. You will fill in the number of pages and the appropriate dates where indicated after you have properly typed your will or had it typed. The use of the notary acknowledgment, although not a strict legal necessity, is strongly recommended. This allows the will to become "self-proving" and the witnesses need not be called upon to testify in court at a later date after your death that they, indeed, signed the will as witnesses. Although a few states have not enacted legislation to allow for the use of this type of sworn and acknowledged testimony to be used in court, the current trend is to allow for its use in probate courts. This saves time, money, and trouble in having your will admitted to *probate* (the court administration of your will) when necessary.

The actual signing of the will by both you and your witnesses will be explained later in this chapter, following the will forms.

Instructions for Will for Married Person with Children (Using Children's Trust)

This will is appropriate for use by a married person with one or more children. There are also provisions in this will for use if the parent has minor children and desires to place the property and assets that may be left to the children into a trust fund. In addition, this will allows a parent to choose a person to act as guardian for any minor children. In most cases, a married person may desire to choose the other spouse as both trustee and guardian for any of their children, although this is not a legal requirement. If the parent has no minor children, the will clauses relating to the children's trust and to guardianship of the children may be deleted. Each spouse/parent must prepare his or her own will. Do not attempt to prepare a joint will for both you and your spouse together.

This will contains the following standard clauses:

- Title Clause
- Identification Clause
- Marital Status Clause
- Identification of Children Clause
- Identification of Grandchildren Clause
- Specific Gifts Clause
- Residuary Clause
- Survivorship Clause
- Executor Clause
- Child Guardianship Clause
- Children's Trust Fund Clause
- Organ Donation Clause
- Funeral Arrangements Clause
- Signature and Self-Proving Clause

Fill in each of the appropriate blanks in this will using the information that you included in your Property and Beneficiary Questionnaires. Cross out any information that is not appropriate to your situation. The necessary information to be filled-in is noted below and should be written into the place where the corresponding number appears in the following will form.

①   Full name of testator
②   Full name of testator (and any other names that you are known by)
③   Full address of testator

④   Spouse's full name (give information on previous marriage, if necessary [see page 61])

⑤ Number of children
⑥ Child's name (repeat for each child)
⑦ Child's address (repeat for each child)
⑧ Child's date of birth (repeat for each child)

⑨ Number of grandchildren (if applicable)
⑩ Grandchild's name (repeat for each grandchild)
⑪ Grandchild's address (repeat for each grandchild)
⑫ Grandchild's date of birth (repeat for each grandchild)

⑬ Complete description of specific gift (repeat for each specific gift)
⑭ Full name of beneficiary (repeat for each specific gift)
⑮ Relationship of beneficiary to testator (repeat for each specific gift)
⑯ Full name of alternate beneficiary (repeat for each specific gift)
⑰ Relationship of alternate beneficiary to testator (repeat for each specific gift)

⑱ Full name of residual beneficiary
⑲ Relationship of residual beneficiary to testator
⑳ Full name of alternate residual beneficiary
㉑ Relationship of alternate residual beneficiary to testator

㉒ Full name of executor
㉓ Relationship of executor to testator
㉔ Full address of executor
㉕ Full name of alternate executor
㉖ Relationship of alternate executor to testator
㉗ Full address of alternate executor

㉘ Full name of guardian of children
㉙ Relationship of guardian of children to testator
㉚ Full address of guardian of children
㉛ Full name of alternate guardian of children
㉜ Relationship of alternate guardian of children to testator
㉝ Full address of alternate guardian of children

㉞ Children's age to be subject to children's trust
㉟ Children's age for end of children's trust (21, 25, or 30 years or older)
㊱ Full name of trustee of children's trust
㊲ Relationship of trustee of children's trust to testator
㊳ Full address of trustee of children's trust
㊴ Full name of alternate trustee of children's trust
㊵ Relationship of alternate trustee of children's trust to testator
㊶ Full address of alternate trustee of children's trust

㊷ Name of funeral home
㊸ Address of funeral home
㊹ Name of cemetery
㊺ Address of cemetery

Number of total pages of will (fill in when will is typed or printed)
Date of signing of will (DO NOT FILL IN YET)
Signature of testator (DO NOT FILL IN YET)
Printed name of testator (DO NOT FILL IN YET)
Date of witnessing of will (DO NOT FILL IN YET)
Signature of witness (repeat for each witness) [DO NOT FILL IN YET]
Printed name of witness (repeat for each witness) [DO NOT FILL IN YET]
Address of witness (repeat for each witness) [DO NOT FILL IN YET]

㊻ Notary Acknowledgment (to be filled in by Notary Public)

Will for Married Person with Children (Using Children's Trust)

Last Will and Testament of ①

I, ② ,
whose address is ③ ,
declare that this is my Last Will and Testament and I revoke all previous wills.

I am married to ④ .

I have ⑤ child(ren) living. His/Her/Their name(s), address(es), and date(s) of birth is/are as follows:
⑥
⑦
⑧

⑥
⑦
⑧

⑥
⑦
⑧

I have ⑨ grandchild(ren) living. His/Her/Their name(s), address(es), and date(s) of birth is/are as follows:
⑩
⑪
⑫

⑩
⑪
⑫

⑩
⑪
⑫

Page ___ of ___ pages   Testator's initials _____

I make the following specific gifts:

I give ⑬ ,
to ⑭ ,
my ⑮ ,
or if not surviving, then to ⑯ ,
my ⑰ .

I give ⑬ ,
to ⑭ ,
my ⑮ ,
or if not surviving, then to ⑯ ,
my ⑰ .

I give ⑬ ,
to ⑭ ,
my ⑮ ,
or if not surviving, then to ⑯ ,
my ⑰ .

I give ⑬ ,
to ⑭ ,
my ⑮ ,
or if not surviving, then to ⑯ ,
my ⑰ .

I give ⑬ ,
to ⑭ ,
my ⑮ ,
or if not surviving, then to ⑯ ,
my ⑰ .

I give ⑬ ,
to ⑭ ,
my ⑮ ,
or if not surviving, then to ⑯ ,
my ⑰ .

I give ⑬ ,
to ⑭ ,
my ⑮ ,
or if not surviving, then to ⑯ ,
my ⑰ .

I give all the rest of my property, whether real or personal, wherever located,
to ⑱ ,
my ⑲ ,
or if not surviving, to ⑳ ,
my ㉑ .

All beneficiaries named in this will must survive me by thirty (30) days to receive any gift under this will. If any beneficiary and I should die simultaneously, I shall be conclusively presumed to have survived that beneficiary for purposes of this will.

I appoint ㉒ ,
my ㉓ ,
of ㉔ ,
as Executor, to serve without bond. If not surviving or otherwise unable to serve,
I appoint ㉕ ,
my ㉖ ,
of ㉗ ,
as Alternate Executor, also to serve without bond. In addition to any powers, authority, and discretion granted by law, I grant such Executor or Alternate Executor any and all powers to perform any acts, in his/her sole discretion and without court approval, for the management and distribution of my estate, including independent administration of my estate.

If a Guardian is needed for my/any of my minor child(ren),
I appoint ㉘ ,
my ㉙ ,
of ㉚ ,
as Guardian of the person(s) and property of my/any of my minor child(ren), to serve without bond. If not surviving, or unable to serve,
I appoint ㉛ ,
my ㉜ ,
of ㉝ ,
as Alternate Guardian, also to serve without bond. In addition to any powers, authority, and discretion granted by law, I grant such Guardian or Alternate Guardian any and all powers to perform any acts, in his/her sole discretion and without court approval, for the management and distribution of the property of my/any of my minor child(ren).

If my/any of my child(ren) is/are under ㉞ years of age, upon my death, I direct that any property that I give him/her/them under this will be held in an individual trust for my/each child(ren), under the following terms, until he/she/each shall reach ㉟ years of age.

Page ___ of ___ pages   Testator's initials _____

In addition, I appoint ㊱ ,
my ㊲ ,
of ㊳ ,
as Trustee of any and all required trusts, to serve without bond. If not surviving, or otherwise unable to serve, then I appoint ㊴ ,
my ㊵ ,
of ㊶ ,
as Alternate Trustee, also to serve without bond. In addition to all powers, authority, and discretion granted by law, I grant such Trustee or Alternate Trustee full power to perform any act, in his/her sole discretion and without court approval, to distribute and manage the assets of any such trust.

In the Trustee's sole discretion, the Trustee may distribute any or all of the principal, income, or both, of any such trust as deemed necessary for the beneficiary's health, support, welfare, and education. Any income not distributed shall be added to the trust principal.

Any such trust shall terminate when the beneficiary reaches the required age, when the beneficiary dies prior to reaching the required age, or when all trust funds have been distributed. Upon termination, any remaining undistributed principal and income shall pass to the beneficiary; or if not surviving, to the beneficiary's heirs; or if none, to the residue of my estate.

I also declare that, pursuant to the Uniform Anatomical Gift Act, I donate any of my body parts and/or organs to any medical institution willing to accept and use them, and I direct my Executor to carry out such donation.

Funeral arrangements have been made with the ㊷ ,
of ㊸ ,
for burial at ㊹ ,
located in ㊺ ,
and I direct my Executor to carry out such arrangements.

I publish and sign this Last Will and Testament, consisting of _____ typewritten pages, on _____ , 20 _____ , and declare that I do so freely, for the purposes expressed, under no constraint or undue influence, and that I am of sound mind and of legal age.

_____
Signature of Testator

_____
Printed Name of Testator

We, the undersigned, being first sworn on oath and under penalty of perjury, state that:

On _____ , 20 _____ , in the presence of all of us, the above-named Testator published and signed this Last Will and Testament, and then at Testator's request, and in Testator's presence, and in each other's presence, we all signed below as witnesses, and we declare, under penalty of perjury, that, to the best of our knowledge, the Testator signed this instrument freely, under no constraint or undue influence, and is of sound mind and legal age.

_____   _____
Signature of Witness #1   Signature of Witness #3

_____   _____
Printed Name of Witness #1   Printed Name of Witness #3

_____   _____
Address of Witness #1   Address of Witness #3

_____
Signature of Witness #2

_____
Printed Name of Witness #2

_____
Address of Witness #2

㊻ Notary Acknowledgment

State of _____
County of _____

On _____ , 20 _____ , _____ ,
the Testator, and _____ , _____ ,
and _____ , the witnesses, personally came before me and, being duly sworn, did state that they are the persons described in the above document and that they signed the above document in my presence as a free and voluntary act for the purposes stated.

_____
Signature of Notary Public

Notary Public, In and for the County of _____
State of _____

My commission expires: _____   Notary Seal

Page ___ of ___ pages   Testator's initials _____

Instructions for Will for Single Person with Children
(Using Children's Trust)

This will is appropriate for use by a single person with one or more children. There are also provisions in this will for use if the parent has minor children and desires to place the property and assets that may be left to the children into a trust fund. In addition, this will allows a parent to choose a person to act as guardian for any minor children. In most cases, a parent may desire to choose the other parent as both trustee and guardian for any of their children, although this is not a legal requirement and may not be the best solution if the parents are divorced. If the parent has no minor children, the will clauses relating to the children's trust and to guardianship of the children may be deleted.

This will contains the following standard clauses:

- Title Clause
- Identification Clause
- Marital Status Clause
- Identification of Children Clause
- Identification of Grandchildren Clause
- Specific Gifts Clause
- Residuary Clause
- Survivorship Clause
- Executor Clause
- Child Guardianship Clause
- Children's Trust Fund Clause
- Organ Donation Clause
- Funeral Arrangements Clause
- Signature and Self-Proving Clause

Fill in each of the appropriate blanks in this will using the information that you included in your Property and Beneficiary Questionnaires. Cross out any information that is not appropriate to your situation. The necessary information to be filled-in is noted below and should be written into the place where the corresponding number appears in the following will form.

(1) Full name of testator
(2) Full name of testator (and any other names that you are known by)
(3) Full address of testator

(Give information on previous marriage, if necessary [see page 61])

④ Number of children
⑤ Child's name (repeat for each child)
⑥ Child's address (repeat for each child)
⑦ Child's date of birth (repeat for each child)

⑧ Number of grandchildren (if applicable)
⑨ Grandchild's name (repeat for each grandchild)
⑩ Grandchild's address (repeat for each grandchild)
⑪ Grandchild's date of birth (repeat for each grandchild)

⑫ Complete description of specific gift (repeat for each specific gift)
⑬ Full name of beneficiary (repeat for each specific gift)
⑭ Relationship of beneficiary to testator (repeat for each specific gift)
⑮ Full name of alternate beneficiary (repeat for each specific gift)
⑯ Relationship of alternate beneficiary to testator (repeat for each specific gift)

⑰ Full name of residual beneficiary
⑱ Relationship of residual beneficiary to testator
⑲ Full name of alternate residual beneficiary
⑳ Relationship of alternate residual beneficiary to testator

㉑ Full name of executor
㉒ Relationship of executor to testator
㉓ Full address of executor
㉔ Full name of alternate executor
㉕ Relationship of alternate executor to testator
㉖ Full address of alternate executor

㉗ Full name of guardian of children
㉘ Relationship of guardian of children to testator
㉙ Full address of guardian of children
㉚ Full name of alternate guardian of children
㉛ Relationship of alternate guardian of children to testator
㉜ Full address of alternate guardian of children

㉝ Children's age to be subject to children's trust
㉞ Children's age for end of children's trust (21, 25, or 30 years or older)
㉟ Full name of trustee of children's trust
㊱ Relationship of trustee of children's trust to testator
㊲ Full address of trustee of children's trust
㊳ Full name of alternate trustee of children's trust
㊴ Relationship of alternate trustee of children's trust to testator
㊵ Full address of alternate trustee of children's trust

④① Name of funeral home
④② Address of funeral home
④③ Name of cemetery
④④ Address of cemetery

Number of total pages of will (fill in when will is typed or printed)
Date of signing of will (DO NOT FILL IN YET)
Signature of testator (DO NOT FILL IN YET)
Printed name of testator (DO NOT FILL IN YET)
Date of witnessing of will (DO NOT FILL IN YET)
Signature of witness (repeat for each witness) [DO NOT FILL IN YET]
Printed name of witness (repeat for each witness) [DO NOT FILL IN YET]
Address of witness (repeat for each witness) [DO NOT FILL IN YET]

④⑤ Notary Acknowledgment (to be filled in by Notary Public)

Will for Single Person with Children
(Using Children's Trust)

Last Will and Testament of ①

I, ② ,
whose address is ③ ,
declare that this is my Last Will and Testament and I revoke all previous wills.

I am not currently married.

I have ④ child(ren) living. His/Her/Their name(s), address(es), and date(s) of birth is/are as follows:

⑤
⑥
⑦

⑤
⑥
⑦

⑤
⑥
⑦

I have ⑧ grandchild(ren) living. His/Her/Their name(s), address(es), and date(s) of birth is/are as follows:

⑨
⑩
⑪

⑨
⑩
⑪

⑨
⑩
⑪

Page ___ of ___ pages   Testator's initials _____

I make the following specific gifts:

I give ⑫ ,
to ⑬ ,
my ⑭ ,
or if not surviving, then to ⑮ ,
my ⑯ .

I give ⑫ ,
to ⑬ ,
my ⑭ ,
or if not surviving, then to ⑮ ,
my ⑯ .

I give ⑫ ,
to ⑬ ,
my ⑭ ,
or if not surviving, then to ⑮ ,
my ⑯ .

I give ⑫ ,
to ⑬ ,
my ⑭ ,
or if not surviving, then to ⑮ ,
my ⑯ .

I give ⑫ ,
to ⑬ ,
my ⑭ ,
or if not surviving, then to ⑮ ,
my ⑯ .

I give ⑫ ,
to ⑬ ,
my ⑭ ,
or if not surviving, then to ⑮ ,
my ⑯ .

I give ⑫ ,
to ⑬ ,
my ⑭ ,
or if not surviving, then to ⑮ ,
my ⑯ .

I give all the rest of my property, whether real or personal, wherever located,
to ⑰ ,
my ⑱ ,
or if not surviving, to ⑲ ,
my ⑳ .

All beneficiaries named in this will must survive me by thirty (30) days to receive any gift under this will. If any beneficiary and I should die simultaneously, I shall be conclusively presumed to have survived that beneficiary for purposes of this will.

I appoint ㉑ ,
my ㉒ ,
of ㉓ ,
as Executor, to serve without bond. If not surviving or otherwise unable to serve,
I appoint ㉔ ,
my ㉕ ,
of ㉖ ,
as Alternate Executor, also to serve without bond. In addition to any powers, authority, and discretion granted by law, I grant such Executor or Alternate Executor any and all powers to perform any acts, in his or her sole discretion and without court approval, for the management and distribution of my estate, including independent administration of my estate.

If a Guardian is needed for my/any of my minor child(ren),
I appoint ㉗ ,
my ㉘ ,
of ㉙ ,
as Guardian of the person and property of my/any of my minor child(ren), to serve without bond. If not surviving, or unable to serve,
I appoint ㉚ ,
my ㉛ ,
of ㉜ ,
as Alternate Guardian, also to serve without bond. In addition to any powers, authority, and discretion granted by law, I grant such Guardian or Alternate Guardian any and all powers to perform any acts, in his/her sole discretion and without court approval, for the management and distribution of the property of my/any of my minor child(ren).

If my/any of my child(ren) is/are under ㉝ years of age, upon my death, I direct that any property that I give him/her/them under this will be held in an individual trust for my/each child(ren), under the following terms, until he/she/each shall reach ㉞ years of age.

Page ___ of ___ pages   Testator's initials _____

In addition, I appoint ㉟ ,

my ㊱ ,

of ㊲ ,

as Trustee of any and all required trusts, to serve without bond. If not surviving, or otherwise unable to serve, then I appoint ㊳ ,

my ㊴ ,

of ㊵ ,

as Alternate Trustee, also to serve without bond. In addition to all powers, authority, and discretion granted by law, I grant such Trustee or Alternate Trustee full power to perform any act, in his/her sole discretion and without court approval, to distribute and manage the assets of any such trust.

In the Trustee's sole discretion, the Trustee may distribute any or all of the principal, income, or both, of any such trust as deemed necessary for the beneficiary's health, support, welfare, and education. Any income not distributed shall be added to the trust principal.

Any such trust shall terminate when the beneficiary reaches the required age, when the beneficiary dies prior to reaching the required age, or when all trust funds have been distributed. Upon termination, any remaining undistributed principal and income shall pass to the beneficiary; or if not surviving, to the beneficiary's heirs; or if none, to the residue of my estate.

I also declare that, pursuant to the Uniform Anatomical Gift Act, I donate any of my body parts and/or organs to any medical institution willing to accept and use them, and I direct my Executor to carry out such donation.

Funeral arrangements have been made with the ㊶ ,

of ㊷ ,

for burial at ㊸ ,

located in ㊹ ,

and I direct my Executor to carry out such arrangements.

I publish and sign this Last Will and Testament, consisting of _____ typewritten pages, on _____ , 20 _____ , and declare that I do so freely, for the purposes expressed, under no constraint or undue influence, and that I am of sound mind and of legal age.

_____   _____
Signature of Testator   Printed Name of Testator

We, the undersigned, being first sworn on oath and under penalty of perjury, state that:

On _____ , 20 _____ , in the presence of all of us, the above-named Testator published and signed this Last Will and Testament, and then at Testator's request, and in Testator's presence, and in each other's presence, we all signed below as witnesses, and we declare, under penalty of perjury, that, to the best of our knowledge, the Testator signed this instrument freely, under no constraint or undue influence, and is of sound mind and legal age.

_____
Signature of Witness #1

_____
Printed Name of Witness #1

_____
Address of Witness #1

_____
Signature of Witness #3

_____
Printed Name of Witness #3

_____
Address of Witness #3

_____
Signature of Witness #2

_____
Printed Name of Witness #2

_____
Address of Witness #2

㊺ Notary Acknowledgment

State of _____
County of _____

On _____ , 20 _____ , _____ , the Testator, and _____ , _____ , and _____ , the witnesses, personally came before me and, being duly sworn, did state that they are the persons described in the above document and that they signed the above document in my presence as a free and voluntary act for the purposes stated.

_____
Signature of Notary Public

Notary Public, In and for the County of _____
State of _____

My commission expires: _____   Notary Seal

Page ___ of ___ pages   Testator's initials _____

Instructions for Will for Married Person with No Children

This will is appropriate for use by a married person with no children or grandchildren. Each spouse must prepare his or her own will. Do not attempt to prepare a joint will for both you and your spouse together.

This will contains the following standard clauses:

- Title Clause
- Identification Clause
- Marital Status Clause
- Specific Gifts Clause
- Residuary Clause
- Survivorship Clause
- Executor Clause
- Organ Donation Clause
- Funeral Arrangements Clause
- Signature and Self-Proving Clause

Fill in each of the appropriate blanks in this will using the information that you included in your Property and Beneficiary Questionnaires. Cross out any information that is not appropriate to your situation. The necessary information to be filled-in is noted below and should be written into the place where the corresponding number appears in the following will form.

①   Full name of testator
②   Full name of testator (and any other names that you are known by)
③   Full address of testator

④   Spouse's full name (give information on previous marriage, if necessary [see page 61])

⑤   Complete description of specific gift (repeat for each specific gift)
⑥   Full name of beneficiary (repeat for each specific gift)
⑦   Relationship of beneficiary to testator (repeat for each specific gift)
⑧   Full name of alternate beneficiary (repeat for each specific gift)
⑨   Relationship of alternate beneficiary to testator (repeat for each specific gift)

⑩   Full name of residual beneficiary
⑪   Relationship of residual beneficiary to testator
⑫   Full name of alternate residual beneficiary
⑬   Relationship of alternate residual beneficiary to testator

⑭ Full name of executor
⑮ Relationship of executor to testator
⑯ Full address of executor
⑰ Full name of alternate executor
⑱ Relationship of alternate executor to testator
⑲ Full address of alternate executor

⑳ Name of funeral home
㉑ Address of funeral home
㉒ Name of cemetery
㉓ Address of cemetery

Number of total pages of will (fill in when will is typed or printed)
Date of signing of will (DO NOT FILL IN YET)
Signature of testator (DO NOT FILL IN YET)
Printed name of testator (DO NOT FILL IN YET)
Date of witnessing of will (DO NOT FILL IN YET)
Signature of witness (repeat for each witness) [DO NOT FILL IN YET]
Printed name of witness (repeat for each witness) [DO NOT FILL IN YET]
Address of witness (repeat for each witness) [DO NOT FILL IN YET]

㉔ Notary Acknowledgment (to be filled in by Notary Public)

Will for Married Person with No Children

Last Will and Testament of ①

I, ② ,
whose address is ③ ,
declare that this is my Last Will and Testament and I revoke all previous wills.

I am married to ④ .

I have no children or grandchildren living.

I make the following specific gifts:

I give ⑤ ,
to ⑥ ,
my ⑦ ,
or if not surviving, then to ⑧ ,
my ⑨ .

I give ⑤ ,
to ⑥ ,
my ⑦ ,
or if not surviving, then to ⑧ ,
my ⑨ .

I give ⑤ ,
to ⑥ ,
my ⑦ ,
or if not surviving, then to ⑧ ,
my ⑨ .

I give ⑤ ,
to ⑥ ,
my ⑦ ,
or if not surviving, then to ⑧ ,
my ⑨ .

Page ___ of ___ pages

Testator's initials _____

I give all the rest of my property, whether real or personal, wherever located,
to ⑩ ,
my ⑪ ,
or if not surviving, to ⑫ ,
my ⑬ .

All beneficiaries named in this will must survive me by thirty (30) days to receive any gift under this will. If any beneficiary and I should die simultaneously, I shall be conclusively presumed to have survived that beneficiary for purposes of this will.

I appoint ⑭ ,
my ⑮ ,
of ⑯ ,
as Executor, to serve without bond. If not surviving or otherwise unable to serve,
I appoint ⑰ ,
my ⑱ ,
of ⑲ ,
as Alternate Executor, also to serve without bond. In addition to any powers, authority, and discretion granted by law, I grant such Executor or Alternate Executor any and all powers to perform any acts, in his/her sole discretion and without court approval, for the management and distribution of my estate, including independent administration of my estate.

I also declare that, pursuant to the Uniform Anatomical Gift Act, I donate any of my body parts and/or organs to any medical institution willing to accept and use them, and I direct my Executor to carry out such donation.

Funeral arrangements have been made with the ⑳ ,
of ㉑ ,
for burial at ㉒ ,
located in ㉓ ,
and I direct my Executor to carry out such arrangements.

I publish and sign this Last Will and Testament, consisting of _____ typewritten pages, on _____ , 20 _____ , and declare that I do so freely, for the purposes expressed, under no constraint or undue influence, and that I am of sound mind and of legal age.

_____   _____
Signature of Testator   Printed Name of Testator

Page ___ of ___ pages   Testator's initials _____

We, the undersigned, being first sworn on oath and under penalty of perjury, state that:

On _____ , 20 _____ , in the presence of all of us, the above-named Testator published and signed this Last Will and Testament, and then at Testator's request, and in Testator's presence, and in each other's presence, we all signed below as witnesses, and we declare, under penalty of perjury, that, to the best of our knowledge, the Testator signed this instrument freely, under no constraint or undue influence, and is of sound mind and legal age.

_____
Signature of Witness #1

_____
Printed Name of Witness #1

_____
Address of Witness #1

_____
Signature of Witness #2

_____
Printed Name of Witness #2

_____
Address of Witness #2

_____
Signature of Witness #3

_____
Printed Name of Witness #3

_____
Address of Witness #3

㉔ Notary Acknowledgment

State of _____
County of _____

On _____ , 20 _____ , _____ , the Testator, and _____ , _____ , and _____ , the witnesses, personally came before me and, being duly sworn, did state that they are the persons described in the above document and that they signed the above document in my presence as a free and voluntary act for the purposes stated.

_____
Signature of Notary Public

Notary Public, In and for the County of _____
State of _____

My commission expires: _____   Notary Seal

Page ___ of ___ pages   Testator's initials _____

Instructions for Will for Single Person with No Children

This will is appropriate for use by a single person with no children or grandchildren. This will contains the following standard clauses:

- Title Clause
- Identification Clause
- Marital Status Clause
- Specific Gifts Clause
- Residuary Clause
- Survivorship Clause
- Executor Clause
- Organ Donation Clause
- Funeral Arrangements Clause
- Signature and Self-Proving Clause

Fill in each of the appropriate blanks in this will using the information that you included in your Property and Beneficiary Questionnaires. Cross out any information that is not appropriate to your situation. The necessary information to be filled-in is noted below and should be written into the place where the corresponding number appears in the following will form.

① Full name of testator
② Full name of testator (and any other names that you are known by)
③ Full address of testator

(Give information on previous marriage, if necessary [see page 61])

④ Complete description of specific gift (repeat for each specific gift)
⑤ Full name of beneficiary (repeat for each specific gift)
⑥ Relationship of beneficiary to testator (repeat for each specific gift)
⑦ Full name of alternate beneficiary (repeat for each specific gift)
⑧ Relationship of alternate beneficiary to testator (repeat for each specific gift)

⑨ Full name of residual beneficiary
⑩ Relationship of residual beneficiary to testator
⑪ Full name of alternate residual beneficiary
⑫ Relationship of alternate residual beneficiary to testator

⑬ Full name of executor
⑭ Relationship of executor to testator
⑮ Full address of executor

⑯ Full name of alternate executor
⑰ Relationship of alternate executor to testator
⑱ Full address of alternate executor

⑲ Name of funeral home
⑳ Address of funeral home
㉑ Name of cemetery
㉒ Address of cemetery

Number of total pages of will (fill in when will is typed or printed)
Date of signing of will (DO NOT FILL IN YET)
Signature of testator (DO NOT FILL IN YET)
Printed name of testator (DO NOT FILL IN YET)
Date of witnessing of will (DO NOT FILL IN YET)
Signature of witness (repeat for each witness) [DO NOT FILL IN YET]
Printed name of witness (repeat for each witness) [DO NOT FILL IN YET]
Address of witness (repeat for each witness) [DO NOT FILL IN YET]

㉓ Notary Acknowledgment (to be filled in by Notary Public)

Will for Single Person with No Children

Last Will and Testament of ①

I, ② ,
whose address is ③ ,
declare that this is my Last Will and Testament and I revoke all previous wills.

I am not currently married.

I have no children or grandchildren living.

I make the following specific gifts:

I give ④ ,
to ⑤ ,
my ⑥ ,
or if not surviving, then to ⑦ ,
my ⑧ .

I give ④ ,
to ⑤ ,
my ⑥ ,
or if not surviving, then to ⑦ ,
my ⑧ .

I give ④ ,
to ⑤ ,
my ⑥ ,
or if not surviving, then to ⑦ ,
my ⑧ .

I give ④ ,
to ⑤ ,
my ⑥ ,
or if not surviving, then to ⑦ ,
my ⑧ .

I give all the rest of my property, whether real or personal, wherever located, to ⑨ ,
my ⑩ ,
or if not surviving, to ⑪ ,
my ⑫ .

All beneficiaries named in this will must survive me by thirty (30) days to receive any gift under this will. If any beneficiary and I should die simultaneously, I shall be conclusively presumed to have survived that beneficiary for purposes of this will.

I appoint ⑬ ,
my ⑭ ,
of ⑮ ,
as Executor, to serve without bond. If not surviving or otherwise unable to serve, I appoint ⑯ ,
my ⑰ ,
of ⑱ ,
as Alternate Executor, also to serve without bond. In addition to any powers, authority, and discretion granted by law, I grant such Executor or Alternate Executor any and all powers to perform any acts, in his/her sole discretion and without court approval, for the management and distribution of my estate, including independent administration of my estate.

I also declare that, pursuant to the Uniform Anatomical Gift Act, I donate any of my body parts and/or organs to any medical institution willing to accept and use them, and I direct my Executor to carry out such donation.

Funeral arrangements have been made with the ⑲ ,
of ⑳ ,
for burial at ㉑ ,
located in ㉒ ,
and I direct my Executor to carry out such arrangements.

I publish and sign this Last Will and Testament, consisting of _____ typewritten pages, on _____ , 20 _____ , and declare that I do so freely, for the purposes expressed, under no constraint or undue influence, and that I am of sound mind and of legal age.

_____   _____
Signature of Testator   Printed Name of Testator

Page ___ of ___ pages   Testator's initials _____

We, the undersigned, being first sworn on oath and under penalty of perjury, state that:

On _____ , 20 _____ , in the presence of all of us, the above-named Testator published and signed this Last Will and Testament, and then at Testator's request, and in Testator's presence, and in each other's presence, we all signed below as witnesses, and we declare under penalty that, to the best of our knowledge, the Testator signed this instrument freely, under no constraint or undue influence, and is of sound mind and legal age.

_____
Signature of Witness #1

_____
Printed Name of Witness #1

_____
Address of Witness #1

_____
Signature of Witness #3

_____
Printed Name of Witness #3

_____
Address of Witness #3

_____
Signature of Witness #2

_____
Printed Name of Witness #2

_____
Address of Witness #2

㉓ Notary Acknowledgment

State of _____
County of _____

On _____ , 20 _____ , _____ , the Testator, and _____ , _____ , and _____ , the witnesses, personally came before me and, being duly sworn, did state that they are the persons described in the above document and that they signed the above document in my presence as a free and voluntary act for the purposes stated.

_____
Signature of Notary Public

Notary Public, In and for the County of _____
State of _____

My commission expires: _____   Notary Seal

Page ___ of ___ pages   Testator's initials _____

Completing and Signing Your Will

Type your entire will on clean white sheets of 8½" x 11" paper. Make sure that there are no corrections or erasures on the final copy. Do not attempt to correct the mistakes on the final copy. If you make a mistake, retype that particular page. After you have prepared your will in the proper form (either retyped or on your computer), you are ready to sign it. *Do not* sign your will however, until you have read this section and have all of the necessary witnesses and Notary Public present. The legal requirements listed in this section regarding the proper *execution* (signing) of your will are extremely important and must not be deviated from in any manner in order for your will to be legally valid. These requirements are not at all difficult to follow, but they must be followed precisely. These formal requirements are what transform your will from a mere piece of paper outlining your wishes into a legal document that grants the power to dispose of your property under court order after your death.

The reasons for the formality of these requirements are twofold: first, by requiring a ceremonial-type signing of the document, it is hoped that the testator is made fully aware of the importance of what he or she is doing; and second, by requiring a formal signing witnessed by other adults, it is hoped that any instances of forgery, fraud, and coercion will be avoided, or at least minimized.

Again, these legal formalities must be observed strictly. *Do not* deviate from these instructions in any way. The formal execution or signing of your will makes it legally valid and failure to properly sign your will renders it invalid. To properly execute your will, follow these few simple steps:

1. Select three witnesses who will be available to assist you in witnessing your will. These persons may be any adults who are not mentioned in the will either as a beneficiary, executor, trustee, or guardian. The witnesses can be friends, neighbors, co-workers, or even strangers. However, it is prudent to choose persons who have been stable members of your community, since they may be called upon to testify in court someday.

2. Arrange for all of your witnesses to meet you at the office or home of a local Notary Public. Many banks, real estate offices, and government offices have notary services and most will be glad to assist you. (The Notary Public may *not* be one of the required three witnesses.)

3. In front of all of the witnesses and the Notary Public, the following should take place in the order shown:

    (a) You should state: "This is my Last Will and Testament, which I am about to sign. I ask that each of you witness my signature." There is no requirement that the witnesses know any of the terms of your will or that they read any of your will. All that is necessary is that they hear you state that it is your will, that you request them to be witnesses, that they observe you sign your will, and that they also sign the will as witnesses in each other's presence.

(b) You will then sign your will in ink, using a pen, at the end of the will in the place indicated, exactly as your name is typewritten on your will. You should also sign your initials on the bottom of each page of your will at this time.

(c) After you have signed, pass your will to the first witness, who should sign in the place indicated and fill in his or her address.

(d) After the first witness has signed, have the will passed to the second witness, who should also sign in the place indicated and fill in his or her address.

(e) After the second witness has signed, have the will passed to the third and final witness, who also signs in the place indicated and fills in his or her address. Throughout this ceremony, you and all of the witnesses must remain together. It is easier if you are all seated around a table or desk.

(f) For the final step, the Notary Public completes the notary acknowledgment section of the will and signs in the space indicated. When this step is completed, your will is a valid legal document and you can be assured that your wishes will be carried out upon the presentation of your will to a probate court upon your death.

Please note that you should *never* under any circumstances sign a duplicate of your will. Once your will has been properly executed following the steps above, you may make photocopies of it. It is a good idea to label any of these photocopies as "COPIES."

Having completed your will according to the instructions above, it is now time to place your will in a safe place. Many people keep their important papers in a safe deposit box at a local bank. Although this is an acceptable place for storing a will, be advised that there are certain drawbacks. Your will should be in a place that is readily accessible at a moment's notice to your executor. Often there are certain unavoidable delays in gaining access to a safe deposit box in an emergency situation. If you are married, and your safe deposit box is jointly held, many of these delays can be avoided. However, even in this situation, some states prevent immediate access to the safe deposit box of a deceased married person. If you decide to keep the original will in your safe deposit box, it is a good idea to keep a copy of your will clearly marked "COPY" at home in a safe but easily-located place, with a note as to where the original will can be found.

An acceptable alternative to a safe deposit box is a home file box or desk that is used for home storage of your important papers. If possible, this storage place should be fire-proof and under lock and key. Wherever you decide to store your will, you will need to inform your chosen executor of its location. The executor will need to obtain the original of your will shortly after your demise to determine if there are any necessary duties that must be looked after without delay; for example, funeral plans or organ donations.

It is also a good practice to store any life insurance policies and a copy of your birth certificate in the same location as your original will. Additionally, it is also prudent to store a copy of your Property Questionnaire and Beneficiary Questionnaire with your will in order to provide your executor with an inventory and location list of your assets and a list of information regarding your heirs and beneficiaries. Any title documents or deeds relating to property that will be transferred under your will may also be stored with your will for the convenience of your executor. One final precaution: If you wish, allow the executor whom you have named to keep a copy of your will. Be careful, however, to be certain that you immediately inform him or her of any new will that you prepare, of any *codicils* (formal changes to your will) you make to your will, or of any decision to *revoke* (cancel) your will. Preparing a codicil to change your will is explained below.

Changing Your Will

In this section, instructions will be given on when and how to change your will and how to *revoke* (cancel) your will. It is most important to follow these instructions carefully should you desire to make *any* changes to your will. Failure to follow these instructions and an attempt to change your will by such methods as crossing out a name or penciling in an addition could have the disastrous effect of voiding portions of, or even perhaps, your entire will. Again, these instructions are not difficult to follow, but are very important to insure that your will remains legally valid.

If you desire to totally revoke your will, there are two acceptable methods:

- Signing a new will that expressly states that you revoke all prior wills. All wills prepared using this book contain such a provision
- Completely destroying, burning, or mutilating your will while it is in your possession, if you actually intend that there be a revocation of your will

Regarding any potential changes that you may wish to make in your will at a later date, you should periodically review the provisions of your will, keeping in mind the following items as they relate to your present situation:

- Have there been any substantial changes in your personal wealth?
- Have there been any changes in your ownership of any property mentioned in your will?

- Have any of the beneficiaries named in your will died or fallen into your disfavor?
- Are any of the persons whom you named as executor, guardian, or trustee in your will no longer willing or able to serve?
- Have you changed the state of your residence?
- Have you been married since the date of your will?
- Have you been divorced since the date of your will?
- Have you had any children since the date of your will?
- Have you adopted any children since the date of your will?
- Do you simply wish to make any corrections, deletions, or additions to any provisions in your will?

If any of these matters apply, you will need to change your will accordingly. Although it is possible to completely rewrite your will to take account of any of these changes, an easier method is to prepare and formally execute a *codicil*, or a written change to a will. Please bear in mind that all of the formalities surrounding the signing of your original will must again be followed for any such changes contained in a codicil to your will in order to be valid.

Never attempt to change any portions of your will by any other method. For example, *do not* attempt to add provisions in the margin of your will, either by typing or writing them in. *Do not* attempt to cross-out any portions of your will. These are not acceptable methods for the alteration of a will and could subject your will to a court battle to determine its subsequent validity.

Following are standard clauses for changing provisions of your will and a general form for a codicil. Insert such changes as are necessary where indicated on the form. Prepare the codicil the same way as you prepared your original will using the following simple list of instructions:

1. Make a photocopy of the codicil form or use the form from the enclosed Forms-on-CD. Using the photocopy or the CD form as a worksheet, fill in the appropriate information for each chosen clause. For the main clause indicating the changes to your will, use one or more of the following phrases. If you wish to change a particular sentence in your will, you should first revoke the original sentence and then add the new sentence. If you merely wish to add new material to the will or revoke a portion of the will, use only one of the phrases below:

I revoke the following sentence of my will:

or,

I add the following sentence to my will:

2. On your photocopy or CD form worksheet version, cross out all extraneous material that will not become a part of your codicil. Carefully reread your entire codicil to be certain that it is exactly as you wish.

3. After making any necessary changes, type or have typed the entire codicil on good quality 8 ½" x 11" typing paper, or prepare the codicil from the Forms-on-CD.

4. After you have completed typing your codicil or having it typed, fill in the total number of pages in the Signature paragraph. *Do not* yet sign your codicil or fill in the date in any of the spaces indicated.

5. Again, proofread your entire codicil very carefully. Be certain that there are no errors. If there are any errors, retype that particular page. *Do not* attempt to correct any errors with type-correcting fluid or tape, or with erasures of any kind. *Do not* cross-out any words and *do not* add anything to the typewritten words using a pen or pencil.

6. When you have a perfect original of your codicil, with no corrections and no additions, staple all of the pages together in the upper left-hand corner. You are now ready to prepare for the *execution* (signing) of your codicil. For signing your codicil, please follow the same instructions from the previous section for signing your will, substituting the statement:

This is my Codicil to my Last Will and Testament that I am about to sign.

As you fill in the information for each clause, keep in mind the following instructions:

Title Clause: The title clause is mandatory for all codicils and must be included. Fill in the name blank with your full legal name. If you have been known by more than one name, use your principal name. Be sure to use the exact same name as you used in the will that you are changing.

Identification Clause: The identification clause is mandatory and must be included in all codicils. In the first blank, include any other names that you are known by. Do this by adding the phrase: "also known as" after your principal full name. For example:

John James Smith, also known as Jimmy John Smith.

In the spaces provided for your residence, use the location of your principal residence; that is, the place where you currently live permanently. Please note the exact date when you signed your current will.

Addition to Will Clause: Use of this clause is optional. Use if you wish to add additional provisions to your will. In the space provided, simply fill in whatever provisions you desired to be added. For example:

I add the following sentence to the [_name of clause_] clause of my will:

Revocation of Paragraph of Will Clause: This clause is optional. Use in those situations where you desire to delete a clause from your original will. Simply indicate which clause it is that you wish to revoke in the space indicated:

I revoke the following clause of my will:

Correction of Will Clause: Use is optional. Use this clause for those situations where you wish to retain a particular clause in your will, but desire to change a portion of it (for example, substitution of the name of a different beneficiary). Where indicated in this clause, type the correct information that you wish to have become part of your will:

I change the [_name of clause_] clause of my will to read as follows:

Signature and Self-Proving Clause: This clause is mandatory. You will fill in the number of pages and the appropriate dates where indicated after you have properly typed your codicil or had it typed. The use of the notary acknowledgment, although not a strict legal necessity, is strongly recommended. This allows the codicil to become "self-proving" and the witnesses need not be called upon to testify in court at a later date (after your death) that they, indeed, signed the codicil as witnesses. Although a few states have not enacted legislation to allow for the use of this type of sworn and acknowledged testimony to be used in court, the current trend is to allow for their use in probate courts. This saves time, money, and trouble in having your codicil admitted to probate when necessary.

The actual signing of the codicil by both you and your witnesses is identical to the method described earlier in the section titled "Completing and Signing Your Will," with the simple use of the term "codicil to my last will and testament." Do *not* sign your codicil until you carefully follow the instructions contained in that section.

Fill in each of the appropriate blanks. Cross out any information that is not appropriate to your situation. The needed information to be filled in is noted below and should be written into the following codicil form in the place where the corresponding number appears.

①　Full name of testator
②　Full name of testator (and any other names that you are known by)
③　Full address of testator

　　Date of signing of codicil (DO NOT FILL IN YET)

④ Complete description of specific change (repeat for each specific change)

Number of total pages of codicil (fill in when codicil is typed or printed)
Date of signing of codicil (DO NOT FILL IN YET)
Signature of testator (DO NOT FILL IN YET)
Printed name of testator (DO NOT FILL IN YET)
Date of witnessing of codicil (DO NOT FILL IN YET)
Signature of witness (repeat for each witness) [DO NOT FILL IN YET]
Printed name of witness (repeat for each witness) [DO NOT FILL IN YET]
Address of witness (repeat for each witness) [DO NOT FILL IN YET]

⑤ Notary Acknowledgment (to be filled in by Notary Public)

Codicil

Codicil to the Last Will and Testament of ①

I, ② ,
whose address is ③ ,
declare that this is a Codicil to my Last Will and Testament, dated
_____ .

I make the following changes to my Last Will and Testament: ④

I republish my Last Will and Testament, dated _____ , as
modified by this Codicil and sign this Codicil, consisting of _____ typewritten pages, on
_____ , 20 _____ , and declare that I do so freely, for the
purposes expressed, under no constraint or undue influence, and that I am of sound mind
and of legal age.

_____   _____
Signature of Testator   Printed Name of Testator

We, the undersigned, being first sworn on oath and under penalty of perjury, state that:

On _____ , 20 _____ in the presence of all of us, the
above-named Testator published and signed this Codicil to said Last Will and Testament,
and then at Testator's request, and in Testator's presence, and in each other's presence, we all
signed below as witnesses, and we declare, under penalty of perjury, that, to the best of our
knowledge, the Testator signed this instrument freely, under no constraint or undue influence,
and is of sound mind and legal age.

Page ____ of ____ pages   Testator's initials _____

_____

Signature of Witness #1

_____

Printed Name of Witness #1

_____

Address of Witness #1

_____

Signature of Witness #3

_____

Printed Name of Witness #3

_____

Address of Witness #3

_____

Signature of Witness #2

_____

Printed Name of Witness #2

_____

Address of Witness #2

⑤ Notary Acknowledgment

State of _____

County of _____

On _____ , 20 _____ , _____ ,
the Testator, and _____ , _____ ,
and _____ , the witnesses, personally came before me and, being
duly sworn, did state that they are the persons described in the above document and that they
signed the above document in my presence as a free and voluntary act for the purposes stated.

_____

Signature of Notary Public

Notary Public, In and for the County of _____
State of _____

My commission expires: _____   Notary Seal

Page ____ of ____ pages   Testator's initials _____

CHAPTER 6
Living Wills

A *living will* is a relatively new legal document which has been made necessary by the advent of recent technological advances in the field of medicine that can allow for the continued existence of a person on advanced life-support systems long after any normal semblance of "life," as many people consider it, has ceased. The inherent problem that is raised by this type of extraordinary medical "life-support" is that the person whose life is being artificially continued by such means may not wish to be kept alive beyond what he or she may consider to be the proper time for his or her life to end. However, since a person in such condition has no method of communicating his or her wishes to the medical or legal authorities in charge, a living will was developed which allows one to make these important decisions in advance of the situation.

As more and more advances are made in the medical field in terms of the ability to prevent "clinical" death, the difficult situations envisioned by a living will are destined to occur more often. The legal acceptance of a living will is currently at the forefront of new laws being added in many states.

Although this living will does not address all possible contingencies regarding terminally ill patients, it does provide a written declaration for the individual to make known his or her or decisions on life-prolonging procedures. A living will declares your wishes not to be kept alive by artificial or mechanical means if you are suffering from a terminal condition and your death would be imminent without the use of such artificial means. A living will provides a legally binding written set of instructions regarding your wishes about this important matter.

In order to qualify for the use of a living will, you must meet the following criteria:

- You must be at least 20 years of age
- You must be of "sound mind" and able to comprehend the nature of your action in signing such a document

If you desire that your life not be prolonged artificially when there is no reasonable chance for recovery and death is imminent, please follow the instructions on the next page for completion of your living will. The entire following form is mandatory. It has been adapted to be valid in all states. Healthcare professionals and physicians will be guided by this expression of your desires concerning life-support.

Preparing and Signing a Living Will

1. Make a photocopy of the entire living will form from this chapter. Using the photocopy or the form from the enclosed Forms-on-CD as a worksheet, please fill in the correct information in the appropriate blanks. On clean, white, 8½" x 11" paper, type or have typed the entire living will exactly as shown with your information added, or complete this form using the Forms-on-CD. Carefully re-read this original living will to be certain that it expresses your desires exactly on this very important matter. When you have a clean, clear original typed version, staple all of the pages together in the upper left-hand corner. *Do not* yet sign this document or fill in the date.

2. You should now assemble three witnesses and a Notary Public to witness your signature. As noted on the document itself, these witnesses should have no connection with you from a healthcare or beneficiary standpoint. Specifically, the witnesses must:

   - Be at least 20 years of age
   - Not be related to you in any manner: by blood, marriage, or adoption
   - Not be your attending physician, or a patient or employee of your attending physician; or a patient, physician, or employee of the healthcare facility in which you may be a patient. However, please see the paragraph below
   - Not be entitled to any portion of your estate upon your death under any laws of intestate succession, under your will, or under any codicil
   - Have no claim against any portion of your estate upon your death
   - Not be directly responsible financially for your medical care
   - Not have signed the living will *for* you, even at your direction
   - Not be paid a fee for acting as a witness

   In addition, please note that several states and the District of Columbia have laws in effect regarding witnesses when the declarant is a patient in a nursing home, boarding facility, hospital, or skilled or intermediate healthcare facility. In those situations, it is advisable to have a patient ombudsman, patient advocate, or the director of the healthcare facility to act as the third witness to the signing of a living will. If you are a resident of a healthcare facility, please ask the facility's legal advisor for the correct procedure.

3. In front of all of the witnesses and the Notary Public, the following should take place in the order shown:

   - You should state: "This is my Living Will which I am about to sign. I ask that each of you witness my signature." There is no requirement that the witnesses know any of the terms of your living will or that they read any of your living will. All that is necessary is that they hear you state that it is your living will, that you request them to be witnesses, that they observe you sign your living will, and that they also sign the living will as witnesses in each other's presence.

- You will then sign your living will exactly as your name is typewritten, at the end of your living will, where indicated, in ink using a pen. After you have signed, pass your living will to the first witness, who should sign where indicated and fill in his or her address.

- After the first witness has signed, have the living will passed to the second witness, who should also sign where indicated. After the second witness has signed, have the living will passed to the third and final witness, who also signs where indicated and fills in his or her address. Throughout this ceremony, you and all of the witnesses must remain together.

- The final step is for the Notary Public to sign in the space indicated. When this step is completed, your living will is a valid legal document. Have several copies made and, if appropriate, deliver a copy to your attending physician to have placed in your medical records file. You may also desire to give copies to the person you have chosen as the executor of your will, to your clergy, and to your spouse or other trusted relative.

Some states require that you periodically re-sign your living will for it to remain valid. Please check with an attorney regarding the particular provisions in your state. *Note*: If you are at all unsure of the correct use of any forms in this chapter, please consult a competent attorney.

Living Will Declaration and Directive to Physicians of _____

I, _____ ,
willfully and voluntarily make known my desire that my life not be artificially prolonged under the circumstances set forth below, and, pursuant to any and all applicable laws in the State of _____ , I declare that:

1. If at any time I should have an incurable injury, disease, or illness which has been certified as a terminal condition by my attending physician and one additional physician, both of whom have personally examined me, and such physicians have determined that there can be no recovery from such condition and my death is imminent, and where the application of life-prolonging procedures would serve only to artificially prolong the dying process, I direct that such procedures be withheld or withdrawn, and that I be permitted to die naturally with only the administration of medication, the administration of nutrition, or the performance of any medical procedure deemed necessary to provide me with comfort, care, or to alleviate pain.

2. If at any time I should have been diagnosed as being in a persistent vegetative state which has been certified as incurable by my attending physician and one additional physician, both of whom have personally examined me, and such physicians have determined that there can be no recovery from such condition, and where the application of life-prolonging procedures would serve only to artificially prolong the dying process, I direct that such procedures be withheld or withdrawn, and that I be permitted to die naturally with only the administration of medication, the administration of nutrition, or the performance of any medical procedure deemed necessary to provide me with comfort, care, or to alleviate pain.

3. In the absence of my ability to give directions regarding my treatment in the above situations, including directions regarding the use of such life-prolonging procedures, it is my intention that this declaration shall be honored by my family, my physician, and any court of law, as the final expression of my legal right to refuse medical and surgical treatment. I declare that I fully accept the consequences for such refusal.

4. If I am diagnosed as pregnant, this document shall have no force and effect during my pregnancy.

5. I direct all persons or entities involved with my healthcare in any manner that the decisions expressed in this document are my freely chosen wishes and I direct that they be carried out to the best of your abilities.

Page ___ of ___ pages   Declarant's initials _____

6. I fully understand my legal rights and the legal ramifications of this document, and I state that I sign this document with a full understanding of the importance and consequences of this declaration. I further state that I am emotionally and mentally competent to make this Declaration and Living Will. No person shall be in any way responsible for the making or placing into effect of this Declaration and Living Will or for carrying out my express directions. I also understand that I may revoke this document at any time.

I publish and sign this Living Will Declaration and Directive to Physicians, consisting of _____ typewritten pages, on _____ , 20 _____ , and declare that I do so freely, for the purposes expressed, under no constraint or undue influence, and that I am of sound mind and of legal age.

_____   _____
Signature of Declarant   Printed Name of Declarant

On _____ , 20 _____ , in the presence of all of us, the above-named Declarant published and signed this Living Will Declaration and Directive to Physicians, and then at the Declarant's request, and in the Declarant's presence, and in each other's presence, we all signed below as witnesses, and we each declare, under penalty of perjury, that, to the best of our knowledge:

1. The Declarant is personally known to me and, to the best of my knowledge, the Declarant signed this instrument freely, under no constraint or undue influence, and is of sound mind and memory and legal age, and is fully aware of the possible consequences of this action.

2. I am at least nineteen (19) years of age and I am not related to the Declarant in any manner; by blood, marriage, or adoption.

3. I am not the Declarant's attending physician, or a patient or employee of the Declarant's attending physician; nor am I a patient, physician, or employee of the healthcare facility in which the Declarant is a patient, unless such person is required or allowed to witness the execution of this document by the laws of the state in which this document is executed.

4. I am not entitled to any portion of the Declarant's estate upon the Declarant's death under the laws of intestate succession of any state or country, nor under the Last Will and Testament of the Declarant or any Codicil to such Last Will and Testament.

5. I have no claim against any portion of the Declarant's estate upon the Declarant's death.

6. I am not directly financially responsible for the Declarant's medical care.

Page ____ of ____ pages   Declarant's initials _____

7. I did not sign the Declarant's signature for the Declarant or at the direction of the Declarant, nor have I been paid any fee for acting as a witness to the execution of this document.

_____   _____
Signature of Witness #1   Signature of Witness #3

_____   _____
Printed Name of Witness #1   Printed Name of Witness #3

_____   _____
Address of Witness #1   Address of Witness #3

_____
Signature of Witness #2

_____
Printed Name of Witness #2

_____
Address of Witness #2

State of _____
County of _____

On _____ , 20 _____ , _____ ,
the Declarant, and _____ , _____ ,
and _____ , the witnesses, personally came before me and, being first sworn on oath and under penalty of perjury, state that, in the presence of all the witnesses, the Declarant published and signed the above Living Will Declaration and Directive to Physicians, and then, at Declarant's request, and in the presence of the Declarant and of each other, each of the witnesses signed as witnesses, and stated that, to the best of their knowledge, the Declarant signed said Living Will Declaration and Directive to Physicians freely, under no constraint or undue influence, and is of sound mind and memory and legal age and fully aware of the potential consequences of this action. The witnesses further state that this affidavit is made at the direction of and in the presence of the Declarant.

_____
Signature of Notary Public

Notary Public, In and for the County of _____
State of _____

My commission expires: _____   Notary Seal

Page ___ of ___ pages   Declarant's initials _____

Instructions for Revocation of Your Living Will

All states that have recognized living wills have provided methods for the easy revocation of them. Since a living will provides authority to medical personnel to withhold life-support technology which will likely result in death to the patient, great care must be taken to insure that a change of mind by the patient is heeded.

If revocation of your living will is an important issue, please refer to Nova Publishing Company's *Living Wills Simplified*, by Dan Sitarz, for the laws pertaining to your state.

For the revocation of a living will, any one of the following methods of revocation is generally acceptable:

- Physical destruction of the living will, such as tearing, burning, or mutilating the document

- A written revocation of the living will by you or by a person acting at your direction. A form for this is provided. You may use two witnesses on this form, although most states do not require the use of witnesses for the written revocation of a living will to be valid

- An oral revocation in the presence of a witness who signs and dates a document confirming a revocation. This oral declaration may take any form. Most states allow for a person to revoke such a document by any indication (even non-verbal) of his or her intent to revoke a living will, regardless of his or her physical or mental condition

To use the Revocation of Living Will form, simply photocopy the form on the next page or use the form on the enclosed Forms-on-CD. Fill in the appropriate information, retype the form, and sign it. In addition, your three witnesses may sign it at the same time.

Revocation of Living Will

I, _____ ,
am the Declarant and maker of a Living Will Declaration and Directive to Physicians,
dated: _____ .

By this written revocation, I hereby entirely revoke such Living Will Declaration and Directive to Physicians and intend that it no longer have any force or effect.

Dated _____ , 20 _____

_____
Signature of Declarant

_____
Printed Name of Declarant

_____   _____
Signature of Witness #1   Signature of Witness #3

_____   _____
Printed Name of Witness #1   Printed Name of Witness #3

_____   _____
Address of Witness #1   Address of Witness #3

_____
Signature of Witness #2

_____
Printed Name of Witness #2

_____
Address of Witness #2

CHAPTER 7
Living Trusts

A *living trust* or revocable trust is a legal document that is used to pass on your assets to your beneficiaries upon your death. Thus, it accomplishes much the same results as a will. Like a will, it is revocable at any time during your life. Also, like a will, it allows you to retain control over your assets during your life and affords no direct tax advantages. However, it does have a few advantages over a will and a few disadvantages, as well.

The main advantage to using a living trust instead of a will is that it allows your assets to be passed to your beneficiaries automatically upon your death, without any delay, probate, court intervention, or lawyer's fees. To many people, this very important advantage outweighs any disadvantages. Another advantage is that it is much more difficult to challenge a living trust in court than it is to challenge a will. Finally, a living trust is a more private document that only needs to be recorded with the county recorder in the event that real estate is transferred with such a trust.

Perhaps the most important disadvantage of using a living trust is the need to actually transfer to the trust all of the property intended to be put in trust. This requirement and the need to keep accurate trust records make the actual mechanics of a living trust more complicated than simply preparing a will.

Even if you decide to use a living trust to pass your assets to your beneficiaries, you will also need to prepare a will. This is because regardless of your best efforts, generally, you will not be able to name each and every item of property that you own. Without a will as a backup, any property not named in the living trust will pass to your closest relatives, or if there are none, the property may be forfeited to the state.

To create a living trust, you will first need to decide what property you wish to place in trust. To do this, you may use the property questionnaire that is provided in Chapter 5: *Basic Wills* for use with a will. Assets that are subject to being sold or discarded regularly should not be put in the trust. Next, you will need to decide who is to receive your assets upon your death. Again, you may use the beneficiary questionnaire that is included in Chapter 5. Finally, you will need to decide if you wish to retain all control over the trust. To achieve this end, you will name yourself as trustee.

Once you have created your living trust, you will need to actually transfer the ownership of all of the assets selected to the trust. This transfer may include obtaining a new title to your car, new bank accounts, and a new deed to any real estate. The new ownership will be in the name of the trust itself, with the name of the trustee specified; for example, *The Jane Smith Revocable Living Trust; Jane Smith, Trustee* might be the name on the deed or title. *Note*: In order to transfer property into your trust, you may need to use an Assignment to Living Trust form for personal property (see below) or a Deed of Trust for real estate (see Chapter 15: *Sale of Real Estate*).

The forms described below can be found on the following pages. *Note*: If you are at all unsure of the correct use of these forms, please consult a competent attorney.

Living Trust: Needed for this form is the following information: the name and address of the *grantor* (the one who is creating the trust), the date the trust will take effect, the name of the *trustee* (the one who will have control over the trust, usually the same person as the grantor), the marital status of the grantor, the name of a successor trustee (usually a spouse, child of legal age, or trusted friend), the name of the state in which you reside, and the signature of the grantor/trustee. The signature on this form should be notarized. This form of trust reserves the right to allow you to cancel or amend this trust at any time.

Schedule of Assets of Living Trust: On this form, you will include a listing of all of the property that you wish to transfer into the trust. (For more information on property, please refer to Chapter 5: *Basic Wills*.) This document should be attached to the living trust when completed. This form needs to be notarized.

Schedule of Beneficiaries of Living Trust: On this form, you will include a list of all of your chosen beneficiaries, alternate beneficiaries, and the trust property that you wish them to receive. You will also choose a residual beneficiary. (For more information on beneficiary choices, refer to Chapter 5). This form must be notarized.

Assignment to Living Trust: This form is used to transfer personal property to the trust. Provide a full description of the property transferred. This form should also be notarized.

Amendment of Living Trust: This form is used to make any changes to the living trust; for example, adding or deleting any of the property listed on the Schedule of Assets or changing a beneficiary on the Schedule of Beneficiaries of Living Trust. Simply fill in the name and address of the grantor/trustee and specify the changes to the trust. The signature on this document should also be notarized.

Revocation of Living Trust: This document is used whenever you desire to terminate the trust. You may do this at any time. To revoke your trust, simply fill in the name and address of the grantor/trustee and the date of the original trust. The signature on this document should also be notarized.

Living Trust of _____

Declaration of Trust

I, _____ , the Grantor of this trust, declare and make this Living Trust on _____ , 20 _____ .

This trust will be known as the _____ Living Trust.

I, _____ , will be Trustee of this trust.

My marital status is that _____ .

Property Transfer

I transfer ownership to this trust of all of the assets that are listed on the attached Schedule of Assets of Living Trust, which is specifically made a part of this trust. I reserve the right to add or delete any of these assets at any time. In addition, I will prepare a separate Deed, Assignment, or any other documents necessary to carry out such transfers. Any additions or deletions to the Schedule of Assets of Living Trust must be written, notarized, and attached to this document to be valid.

Grantor's Rights

Until I die, I retain all rights to all income, profits, and control of the trust property. If my principal residence is transferred to this trust, I retain the right to possess and occupy it for my life, rent-free and without charge. I will remain liable for all taxes, insurance, maintenance, related costs, and expenses. The rights that I retain are intended to give me a beneficial interest in my principal residence such that I do not lose any eligibility that I may have for a state homestead exemption for which I am otherwise qualified.

Successor Trustee

Upon my death or if it is certified by a licensed physician that I am physically or mentally unable to manage this trust and my financial affairs, then I appoint

_____ ,

address:

as Successor Trustee, to serve without bond and without compensation. If this Successor Trustee is not surviving or otherwise unable to serve, I appoint

_____ ,

address:

as Alternate Successor Trustee, also to serve without bond and without compensation. The Successor Trustee or Alternative Successor Trustee shall not be liable for any actions taken in good faith. References to "Trustee" in this document shall include any Successor or Alternative Successor Trustees.

Trustee's Powers

In addition to any powers, authority, and discretion granted by law, I grant the Trustee any and all powers to perform any acts, in his or her sole discretion and without court approval, for the management and distribution of this trust. I intend the Trustee to have the same power and authority to manage and distribute the trust assets as an individual owner has over his or her own wholly owned property.

Additional Trustee Powers

The Trustee's powers include, but are not limited to: the power to sell trust property, borrow money, and encumber that property, specifically including trust real estate, by mortgage, deed of trust, or other method; the power to manage trust real estate as if the Trustee were the absolute owner of it, including the power to lease or grant options to lease the property, make repairs or alterations, and insure against loss; the power to sell or grant options for the sale or exchange of any trust property, including stocks, bonds, and any other form of security; the power to invest trust property in property of any kind, including but not limited to bonds, notes, mortgages, and stocks; the power to receive additional property from any source and add to any trust created by this trust; the power to employ and pay reasonable fees to accountants, lawyers, or investment consultants for information or advice relating to the trust; the power to deposit and hold trust funds in both interest-bearing and non-interest-bearing accounts; the power to deposit funds in a bank or other accounts uninsured by FDIC coverage; the power to enter into electronic funds transfer or safe deposit arrangements with financial institutions; the power to continue any business of the Grantor; and the power to institute or defend legal actions concerning the trust or Grantor's affairs.

Incapacitation

Should the Successor Trustee or Alternative Successor Trustee assume management of this trust during the lifetime of the Grantor, the Successor Trustee or Alternative Successor Trustee shall manage the trust solely for the proper healthcare, support, maintenance, comfort, and/or welfare of the Grantor, in accordance with the Grantor's accustomed manner of living.

Termination of Trust

Upon my death, this trust shall become irrevocable. The Successor Trustee shall then pay my valid debts, last expenses, and estate taxes from the assets of this trust. The Successor Trustee shall then distribute the remaining trust assets in the manner shown on the attached Schedule of Beneficiaries of Living Trust which is specifically made a part of this trust. Any additions or deletions to the Schedule of Beneficiaries of Living Trust must be written, notarized, and attached to this document to be valid.

Survivorship

All beneficiaries named in the Schedule of Beneficiaries of Living Trust must survive me by thirty (30) days to receive any gift under this living trust. If any beneficiary and I should die simultaneously, I shall be conclusively presumed to have survived that beneficiary for purposes of this living trust.

Amendments and Revocations

I reserve the right to amend any or all of this trust at any time. The amendments must be written, notarized, and attached to this document to be valid. I also reserve the right to revoke this trust at any time. A revocation of this trust must be written, notarized, and attached to this document to be valid.

Governing Law

This trust, containing _____ typewritten pages, was created on the date noted above and will be governed under the laws of the State of _____ .

Signature

_____   _____
Signature of Grantor   Printed Name of Grantor

Notary Acknowledgment

State of _____
County of _____

On _____ , 20 _____ , _____
came before me personally and, under oath, stated that he or she is the person described in the above document and he or she signed the above document in my presence. I declare under penalty of perjury that the person whose name is subscribed to this instrument appears to be of sound mind and under no duress, fraud, or undue influence.

_____
Signature of Notary Public

Notary Public, In and for the County of _____
State of _____

My commission expires: _____   Notary Seal

Schedule of Assets of Living Trust

This Schedule of Assets of Living Trust is made on _____ , 20 _____ , by _____ , the Grantor, to the _____ Living Trust dated _____ , 20 _____ .

All Grantor's right, title, and interest in the following property shall be the property of the trust:

_____   _____
Signature of Grantor   Printed Name of Grantor

State of _____
County of _____

On _____ , 20 _____ , _____ came before me personally and, under oath, stated that he or she is the person described in the above document and he or she signed the above document in my presence. I declare under penalty of perjury that the person whose name is subscribed to this instrument appears to be of sound mind and under no duress, fraud, or undue influence.

_____
Signature of Notary Public

Notary Public, In and for the County of _____
State of _____

My commission expires: _____   Notary Seal

Schedule of Beneficiaries of Living Trust

This Schedule of Beneficiaries is made on _____ , 20 _____ , by
_____ , the Grantor, to the
_____ Living Trust dated
_____ .

Upon the death of the Grantor of the trust and the payment of all debts, taxes, and liabilities of the Grantor, the Successor Trustee shall distribute the remaining assets of the Trust as follows:

To _____ ,
address:

my _____ , or if not surviving, to
_____ ,
address:

my _____ , the following trust assets shall be distributed:

All the rest and residue of the trust assets shall be distributed to

_____ ,

address:

my _____ , or if not surviving, to

_____ ,

address:

my _____ .

If any of the beneficiaries named on this Schedule of Beneficiaries is subject to the terms of any children's trust in the main trust document to which this Schedule pertains, then any property distributed to such beneficiary shall be subject to the terms of any such children's trust.

_____

Signature of Grantor

_____

Printed Name of Grantor

State of _____
County of _____

On _____ , 20 _____ , _____
came before me personally and, under oath, stated that he or she is the person described in the above document and he or she signed the above document in my presence. I declare under penalty of perjury that the person whose name is subscribed to this instrument appears to be of sound mind and under no duress, fraud, or undue influence.

_____

Signature of Notary Public

Notary Public, In and for the County of _____
State of _____

My commission expires: _____   Notary Seal

Assignment to Living Trust

This Assignment to Living Trust is made on _____ , 20 _____ , between
_____ , the Grantor, and the
_____ Living Trust dated
_____ , 20 _____ .

The Grantor transfers and conveys possession, ownership, and all right, title, and interest in the following property to the Living Trust:

The Grantor warrants that he or she owns this property and that he or she has the full authority to transfer and convey the property to the Living Trust. Grantor also warrants that the property is transferred free and clear of all liens, indebtedness, or liabilities.

Signed and delivered to the Living Trust on the above date.

_____   _____
Signature of Grantor   Printed Name of Grantor

State of _____
County of _____

On _____ , 20 _____ , _____
came before me personally and, under oath, stated that he or she is the person described in the above document and he or she signed the above document in my presence. I declare under penalty of perjury that the person whose name is subscribed to this instrument appears to be of sound mind and under no duress, fraud, or undue influence.

_____
Signature of Notary Public

Notary Public, In and for the County of _____
State of _____

My commission expires: _____   Notary Seal

Amendment of Living Trust

This Amendment of Living Trust is made on _____ , 20 _____ , by _____ , the Grantor, to the _____ Living Trust dated _____ , 20 _____ .

The Grantor modifies the original trust as follows:

All other terms and conditions of the original Living Trust remain in effect without modification. This Amendment, including the original Living Trust, is the entire Living Trust as of this date. The Grantor has signed this Amendment on the date specified at the beginning of this Amendment.

_____

Signature of Grantor

_____

Printed Name of Grantor

State of _____
County of _____

On _____ , 20 _____ , _____ came before me personally and, under oath, stated that he or she is the person described in the above document and he or she signed the above document in my presence. I declare under penalty of perjury that the person whose name is subscribed to this instrument appears to be of sound mind and under no duress, fraud, or undue influence.

_____

Signature of Notary Public

Notary Public, In and for the County of _____
State of _____

My commission expires: _____   Notary Seal

Revocation of Living Trust

On this date _____ , 20 _____ ,
I, _____ , the Grantor, fully and
completely revoke the _____ Living
Trust dated _____ , 20 _____ . All property that is held in trust shall
be returned to the Grantor as my sole property.

_____
Signature of Grantor

_____
Printed Name of Grantor

State of _____
County of _____

On _____ , 20 _____ , _____
came before me personally and, under oath, stated that he or she is the person described in
the above document and he or she signed the above document in my presence. I declare under
penalty of perjury that the person whose name is subscribed to this instrument appears to be
of sound mind and under no duress, fraud, or undue influence.

_____
Signature of Notary Public

Notary Public, In and for the County of _____
State of _____

My commission expires: _____   Notary Seal

CHAPTER 8
Premarital Agreements

A *premarital* (or prenuptial) *agreement* is a specific type of contract between two persons who are intending to marry. This agreement is entered into in order to spell out the effect of the couple's forthcoming marriage on their individual property and financial situations. A premarital agreement is, essentially, an agreement to alter the general legal effect of marriage.

In the United States, there are two general sets of rules that apply to the ownership of marital property. Under the laws of the community property states of Alaska, Arizona, California, Idaho, Louisiana, Nevada, New Mexico, Texas, Washington, and Wisconsin, all property owned by spouses is divided into two distinct classes: *separate* property and *community* property. Separate property is generally described as consisting of three types of property:

- Property that each spouse owned individually prior to their marriage
- Property that each spouse acquired by individual gift, either before or during the marriage (gifts given to both spouses together or gifts given by one spouse to the other are generally considered community property)
- Property that each spouse acquired by inheritance (legally referred to as "by bequest, descent, or devise"), either before or during the marriage

In community property states, all marital property that is not separate property is referred to as community property. This includes anything that is not separate property that either spouse earned or acquired at any time during the marriage. The property acquired during the marriage is considered community property regardless of whose name may be on the title to the property, and regardless of who actually paid for the property (unless it was paid for entirely with one spouse's separate property funds and remains separate). *Note*: Alaska allows spouses to create community property by mutual agreement.

The other 40 states follow what is referred to as the *common-law* method of marital property ownership. This method has distinct similarities to the community property system and yet is different in many respects. In common-law jurisdictions, certain marital property is subject to division by the judge upon divorce. Which property is subject to division varies somewhat from state to state but generally follows two basic patterns. The most common method of classifying property in common-law states closely parallels the method used in community property states. Property is divided into two basic classes: *separate* or *non-marital* property and *marital* property. What constitutes property in each class is very similar to the definitions in community property states. This method of property division is termed *equitable distribution*.

The second method for distribution that is used in several states is to make *all* of a couple's property subject to division upon divorce. Regardless of whether the property was obtained by gift, by inheritance, or was brought into the marriage, and regardless of whose name is on the title or deed, the property may be apportioned to either spouse depending upon the decision of the judge. There is no differentiation between marital, non-marital, or separate property. The property is still divided on a basis which attempts to achieve a general fairness, but all of a couple's property is available for such distribution. Some states use a hybrid of the above two methods.

The use of a premarital agreement can effectively alter the classification of a spouse's property that is brought into a marriage. Thus, with the use of a premarital agreement, the potential spouses can agree that all of their property that they bring into a marriage will remain as their own separate property throughout the marriage and will not be subject to any division upon eventual divorce. A premarital agreement of this type makes a couple's property rights regarding property brought to a marriage similar to that of community property states and those common-law states that follow similar laws regarding separate and marital property.

The premarital agreement in this book also provides that the potential spouses waive forever any and all rights that they may have to alimony or claims of support that would have to be provided out of any property that is in existence as of the date of the premarital agreement. Any property that is acquired during the marriage, however, will remain subject to division in the event of a divorce.

Please use the property questionnaire that is included in Chapter 9: *Marital Settlement Agreements* to specify what property each potential spouse actually owns prior to the marriage. That questionnaire should then be used to fill in the information detailing the property ownership on the premarital agreement. *Note*: If you are at all unsure of the correct use of any forms in this chapter, please consult a competent attorney.

Premarital Agreement

This agreement is made on _____ , 20 _____ , between
_____ ,
address:

and _____ ,
address:

We intend to be married on _____ , 20 _____ , County of
_____ , State of _____ .

We both desire to settle by agreement the ownership rights of all of our property that we currently own and our rights to alimony, spousal support, or maintenance.

THEREFORE, in consideration of our mutual promises, and other good and valuable consideration, we agree as follows:

We agree that the following property of _____ shall be his or her sole and separate property:

We agree that the following property of _____ shall be his or her sole and separate property:

We agree that the above listed property shall remain their own separate and personal estate, including any rents, interest or profits which may be earned on such property. This property shall forever remain free and clear of any claim by the other person. Each person shall have the right to control, sell, or give away their own separate property as if they were not married. We both agree to waive any rights or claims that we may have now or in the future to receive any distribution of any of the other's separate property in the event of divorce or dissolution of marriage.

However, in the event of divorce or dissolution of marriage, any marital property which is acquired after marriage will be subject to division, either by agreement between us or by a judicial determination.

After careful consideration of our circumstances and all of the other terms of this agreement, we both agree to waive any rights or claims that we may have now or in the future to receive alimony, maintenance, or spousal support from any separate property of the other spouse in the event of divorce or dissolution of marriage. We both fully understand that we are forever giving up any rights that we may have to alimony, maintenance, or spousal support from any separate property of the other spouse in the event of divorce or dissolution of marriage.

We have prepared this agreement cooperatively and each of us has fully and honestly disclosed to the other the extent of our assets.

We each understand that we have the right to representation by independent counsel. We each fully understand our rights and we each consider the terms of this agreement to be fair and reasonable.

Both of us agree to execute and deliver any documents, make any endorsements, and do any and all acts that may be necessary or convenient to carry out all of the terms of this agreement.

We agree that this document is intended to be the full and entire premarital agreement between us and should be interpreted and governed by the laws of the State of _____ .

We also agree that every provision of this agreement is expressly made binding upon the heirs, assigns, executors, administrators, successors in interest, and representatives of each of us.

Signed and dated this day _____ , 20 _____

_____   _____
Signature   Signature

_____   _____
Printed Name   Printed Name

_____   _____
Signature of Witness #1   Signature of Witness #2

_____   _____
Printed Name of Witness #1   Printed Name of Witness #2

_____   _____
Address of Witness #1   Address of Witness #2

State of _____
County of _____

On _____ , 20 _____ , _____
and _____ came before me personally and, under oath, stated that they are the persons described in the above document and they signed the above document in my presence. I declare under penalty of perjury that the persons whose names are subscribed to this instrument appear to be of sound mind and under no duress, fraud, or undue influence.

_____
Signature of Notary Public

Notary Public, In and for the County of _____
State of _____

My commission expires: _____   Notary Seal

CHAPTER 9
Marital Settlement Agreements

For many people, separation is the first step in the divorce process. You and your spouse may decide to separate under the terms of a *marital settlement agreement* (separation agreement) or you may wish to seek an actual legal separation from a court. A legal court-ordered separation is slightly different than a separation by agreement. Legal court-ordered separations are not provided for in all states. However, a marital separation by mutual agreement is recognized and honored in every state. However, neither a court-ordered separation nor a separation agreement will legally end the marriage. Only a divorce can do that.

The marital settlement agreement that you prepare using this book will cover all of the terms of an eventual divorce. Included in your agreement will be all of the decisions that you and your spouse make regarding how your property and bills are divided and whether either of you should get alimony. This agreement, when signed by you and your spouse, will become a valid legal contract that will be enforceable in a court of law if either you or your spouse violate its terms. The marital settlement agreement in this book is designed for use only by couples who do *not* have any children.

There are two general sets of rules that apply to the division of property upon divorce in the United States. There are 10 *community property* states that essentially view all of the property obtained during a marriage as being owned equally by the spouses: Alaska, Arizona, California, Idaho, Louisiana, Nevada, New Mexico, Texas, Washington, and Wisconsin. *Note*: Alaska allows spouses to create community property by mutual agreement. All of the other states are known as *common-law* states. In these states, a couple's property is subject to being divided on a more or less fair or equitable basis upon divorce.

The law in community property states generally holds that all property that a couple obtained while they were married should be shared equally by the spouses. Marriage is viewed essentially as an equal business partnership. Property owned by spouses in these states is divided into two distinct classes: *separate* property and *community* property. Separate property is generally described as consisting of three types of property:

- Property that each spouse owned individually prior to their marriage
- Property that each spouse acquired by individual gift, either before or during the marriage (gifts given to both spouses together or gifts given by one spouse to the other are generally considered community property)

- Property that each spouse acquired by inheritance (legally referred to as "by bequest, descent, or devise"), either before or during the marriage

In community property states, all marital property that is not separate property is referred to as community property. This includes anything that is not separate property that either spouse earned or acquired at any time during the marriage. The property acquired during the marriage is considered community property regardless of whose name may be on the title to the property and regardless of who actually paid for the property (unless it was paid for entirely with one spouse's separate property funds and remains separate). All of a couple's bills and obligations that are incurred during a marriage are also considered community property and are to be divided equally upon divorce. A few states, however, consider educational loans for one spouse to be a separate debt and not to be shared by the other spouse upon divorce.

Most community property states require an equal division of all community property or start with a presumption that an *equal* division is the fairest method, although even these states will allow some leeway from an exact 50-50 division depending on the facts of the case. The remaining community property states provide for an *equitable* division of the community property. In this situation, equitable is defined to mean "fair and just."

In the other 40 common-law-type states, there are two methods for property division. There are states that abide by what is known as an *equitable distribution* method of property division. This method has distinct similarities to the community property system and yet is different in many respects. In equitable distribution jurisdictions, certain marital property is subject to division by the judge upon divorce. Which property is subject to division varies somewhat from state to state but generally follows two basic patterns. The most common method of classifying property in equitable distribution states closely parallels the method used in community property states. Property is divided into two basic classes: *separate* or *non-marital* property and *marital* property. What constitutes property in each class is very similar to the definitions in community property states.

The second method for distribution that is used in other states is to make *all* of a couple's property subject to division upon divorce. Regardless of whether the property was obtained by gift, by inheritance, or was brought into the marriage, and regardless of whose name is on the title or deed, the property may be apportioned to either spouse depending upon the decision of the judge. There is no differentiation between marital, non-marital, or separate property. The property is still divided on a basis which attempts to achieve a general fairness, but all of a couple's property is available for such distribution. Some states use a hybrid of the two methods above. For detailed information on state-specific property division laws, please see Nova Publishing Company's *Divorce Yourself: The National No-Fault Divorce Kit*, by Dan Sitarz.

On the following pages you will find several questionnaires, a checklist, and worksheet that cover basic personal information as well as information regarding your property and incomes. These forms can also be found in the enclosed Forms-on-CD. By filling in these questionnaires, you will be able to have in front of you all of the necessary and relevant information needed to prepare your agreement. Following the questionnaires, checklist, and worksheet, you will find a Marital Settlement Agreement that may be filled in with the information from the previous questionnaires, checklist, and worksheet. Finally, there is a Financial Statement form. Each spouse will need to fill in a copy of this form and the completed forms should be attached to the completed Marital Settlement Agreement. If you and your spouse have children or if further information regarding marital settlement agreements or divorce is necessary, please consult Nova Publishing Company's *Divorce Yourself: The National No-Fault Divorce Kit*, by Daniel Sitarz. *Note*: If you are at all unsure of the correct use of any forms in this chapter, please consult a competent attorney.

Preliminary Questionnaire

Wife's full name: _____

Wife's former or maiden name: _____

Does wife desire to use her former name? _____

Wife's social security number: _____

Wife's date of birth: _____

Wife's present address:

_____

_____

Wife's future address (if known):

_____

_____

Date future address is valid: _____

Wife's present phone number: _____

Wife's present occupation: _____

Wife's present place of employment:

_____

_____

Wife's general health:

_____

_____

_____

_____

Was wife previously married? _____

    If YES, how was marriage terminated (divorce, death, etc.)?

_____

_____

_____

Husband's full name: _____

Husband's social security number: _____

Husband's date of birth: _____

Husband's present address:

_____

_____

Husband's future address (if known):

_____

_____

Date future address is valid: _____

Husband's present phone number: _____

Husband's present occupation: _____

Husband's present place of employment:

_____

_____

Husband's general health:

_____

_____

_____

_____

Was husband previously married? _____

   If YES, how was marriage terminated (divorce, death, etc.)?

_____

_____

_____

Full address(es) where husband and wife have lived during the past 12 months:

_____

_____

_____

_____

Date of marriage: _____

Place of marriage:

_____

_____

Are you and your spouse separated? _____

   If YES, on what date did you separate? _____

Have you previously separated at any time? _____

   If YES, on what dates and for how long?

_____

_____

_____

_____

Names and birthdates of any children of this marriage (born or adopted):

_____

_____

_____

_____

_____

_____

Document Checklist

The following is a listing of various documents that may be necessary during your divorce. The list is as comprehensive as possible and many of the documents may not apply to your individual situation. If you have the documents listed in your possession, assemble them into one place and make a note of that fact on this list. If your spouse has the documents, request that he or she do the same. If you know that the document exists, but do not have access to it, make a note to that effect on this list.

- ❑ Wife's birth certificate:
- ❑ Husband's birth certificate:
- ❑ Immigration and naturalization documents:
- ❑ Marriage license:
- ❑ Birth certificates of any children:
- ❑ Any written agreements between wife and husband:
- ❑ Social Security cards:
- ❑ Documents relating to any prior marriage:
- ❑ All documents relating to income, expenses, and property:
  - ❑ Federal, state, and local income tax returns:
  - ❑ Payroll stubs and W-2 Forms:
  - ❑ Records regarding any other income:
  - ❑ Records regarding monthly living expenses:
  - ❑ Pension and retirement plan policies and records:
  - ❑ Stock option and profit-sharing plans and records:
  - ❑ Personal financial statements:
  - ❑ Business tax returns:
  - ❑ Business financial statements:
  - ❑ Deeds to any real estate:
  - ❑ Mortgages or deeds of trust for any real estate:
  - ❑ Copies of any leases:
  - ❑ Checking account statements:
  - ❑ Savings account statements and passbooks:
  - ❑ Certificates of Deposit:
  - ❑ Stock certificates and bonds:

- ❏ Securities stockbroker account statements:
- ❏ Titles to cars, boats, motorcycles, etc.:
- ❏ Any outstanding loan documents:
- ❏ Credit card records:
- ❏ Records of any other debts:
- ❏ Life insurance policies:
- ❏ Health insurance policies:
- ❏ Auto insurance policies:
- ❏ Homeowner's insurance policy:
- ❏ Other insurance policies:
- ❏ Inventory of contents of safe deposit boxes:
- ❏ Appraisals of any property:
- ❏ Records of any gifts or inheritances:
- ❏ Any other important documents:

Marital Property Questionnaire

Real Estate

Family Home

Do you lease a home or apartment? _____
   If YES, how much time is left on the lease? _____
Do you own your own home? _____
   If YES, what is the address? _____
   _____

When was it purchased? _____
   Was this before or during the marriage? _____
Whose money was used for the down payment? _____
Whose name(s) is on the deed? _____
How much was the down payment? .... $ _____
What was the original purchase price? .... $ _____
What is the present market value? .... $ _____
How much is left unpaid on the mortgage? .... $ _____
What is the equity (market value minus mortgage balance)? .... $ _____
How much is the monthly mortgage payment? .... $ _____
How much are the taxes? .... $ _____
How much is the homeowner's insurance? .... $ _____
Have there been any major improvements made since its purchase? _____
   If YES, please describe when and what improvements were made:

   _____
   What was the total cost? .... $ _____
   Whose money was used? _____

List the actual legal description of the home here (taken directly off the deed or mortgage:

_____
_____

Other Real Estate

What is the address?

_____

When was it purchased? _____
   Was this before or during the marriage? _____
Whose money was used for the down payment? _____

Whose name(s) is on the deed? _____

_____

How much was the down payment? .... $ _____
What was the original purchase price? .... $ _____
What is the present market value? .... $ _____
How much is left unpaid on the mortgage? .... $ _____
What is the equity (market value minus mortgage balance)? .... $ _____
How much is the monthly mortgage payment? .... $ _____
How much are the taxes? .... $ _____
How much is the insurance? .... $ _____
Is there any rental income? .... $ _____
Have there been any major improvements made since its purchase? _____
　　If YES, please describe when and what improvements were made: _____

　　_____

　　What was the total cost? .... $ _____
　　Whose money was used? _____

_____
List the actual legal description of the property here (taken directly off the deed or mortgage):
_____
_____

Personal Property

The term "owner" refers to the person in whose name the account, stock, bond, etc. is held.
If jointly held, write "joint."

Bank Accounts

Savings Accounts
Bank: _____
Account number _____
Owner: _____
Amount .... $ _____

Bank: _____
Account number _____
Owner: _____
Amount .... $ _____

Checking Accounts
Bank: _____
Account number _____
Owner: _____
Amount .... $ _____

Bank: _____

Account number _____

Owner: _____

Amount .... $ _____

Certificates of Deposit

Bank: _____

Account number _____

Owner: _____

Amount .... $ _____

Bank: _____

Account number _____

Owner: _____

Amount .... $_____

Money Market Accounts

Bank: _____

Account number _____

Owner: _____

Amount .... $ _____

Stocks

Company: _____

CUSIP number _____

Owner: _____

Number of shares: _____

Annual dividend .... $ _____

Value .... $ _____

Bonds

Company: _____

CUSIP number _____

Owner: _____

Number of shares: _____

Annual interest .... $ _____

Value .... $ _____

Company: _____

CUSIP number _____

Owner: _____

Number of shares: _____

Annual interest .... $ _____

Value .... $ _____

Names and addresses of your and your spouse's stockbrokers:

_____

_____

_____

_____

_____

Income Tax

Did you file a joint return for the last tax year? _____

Is there a tax or refund due? _____

How much state ☐ tax or ☐ refund? .... $ _____

How much federal ☐ tax or ☐ refund? .... $ _____

How much local ☐ tax or ☐ refund? .... $ _____

Other Personal Property

Car

Year: _____

Make and model: _____

Who has possession? _____

Whose name is on title? _____

License plate number and state of registration: _____

Payment .... $ _____

Amount of car loan unpaid .... $ _____

Value .... $ _____

Car

Year: _____

Make and model: _____

Who has possession? _____

Whose name is on title? _____

License plate number and state of registration: _____

Payment .... $ _____

Amount of car loan unpaid .... $ _____

Value .... $ _____

Other Vehicles (Boats, Campers, Motorcycles, etc.)
Describe:

_____

_____

_____

Who has possession? _____

Value .... $ _____

Describe:

_____

_____

_____

Who has possession? _____

Value .... $ _____

Music System
Describe: _____

_____

Who has possession? _____

Value .... $ _____

Jewelry
Describe: _____

_____

Who has possession? _____

Value .... $ _____

Tools
Describe: _____

_____

Who has possession? _____

Value .... $ _____

Sporting Goods
Describe: _____

_____

Who has possession? _____

Value .... $ _____

Furniture
Describe: _____

_____

Who has possession? _____

Value .... $ _____

Describe: _____

_____

Who has possession? _____

Value .... $ _____

Appliances

Describe: _____

_____

Who has possession? _____

Value .... $ _____

Describe: _____

_____

Who has possession? _____

Value .... $ _____

Other Property

Describe: _____

_____

Who has possession? _____

Value .... $ _____

Describe: _____

_____

Who has possession? _____

Value .... $ _____

Business Assets (Corporations, Partnerships, Proprietorships)

Description: _____

Location: _____

_____

Who has ownership? _____

Value .... $ _____

Description: _____

Location: _____

_____

Who has ownership? _____

Value .... $ _____

Retirement/Pension/Profit-Sharing/Stock Option Plans

IRA Accounts
Bank or broker: _____
Account number _____
Owner:_____
Amount .... $ _____

Bank or broker: _____
Account number _____
Owner:_____
Amount .... $ _____

Retirement Funds
Company: _____
Account number _____
Whose fund? _____
Value .... $ _____

Company: _____
Account number _____
Whose fund? _____
Value .... $ _____

Profit-Sharing Plan
Company: _____
Account number _____
Whose fund? _____
Value .... $ _____

Stock Option Plan
Company: _____
Account number _____
Whose fund? _____
Value .... $ _____

Pension Plan
Company: _____
Account number _____
Whose fund? _____
Value .... $ _____

Insurance

Life Insurance
Company: _____
On whose life: _____
Beneficiary: _____
Premium .... $ _____
Cash value .... $ _____

(On children) Company: _____
On whose life: _____
Beneficiary: _____
Premium .... $ _____
Cash value .... $ _____

Medical Insurance
Company: _____
On whom: _____
Amount .... $ _____
Premium .... $ _____

(On children) Company: _____
On whom: _____
Amount .... $ _____
Premium .... $ _____

Disability Insurance
Company: _____
On whom: _____
Amount .... $ _____
Premium .... $ _____

Auto Insurance
Company: _____
Which car? _____
Amount .... $ _____
Premium .... $ _____

Homeowner's Insurance
Company: _____
Property address:

_____
_____
Amount .... $ _____
Premium .... $ _____

Other Insurance

Company: _____

What purpose? _____

Amount .... $ _____

Premium .... $ _____

Separate Property

The term "separate property" generally refers to the property that each spouse held invididually prior to the marriage and any property acquired individually by each spouse by gift or inheritance.

Was the amount of separate personal property that you or your spouse owned at the time of your marriage valued at over $1,000.00? _____

If YES, list all specific property owned prior to marriage that is still owned (note who owns each item and its value). List property here even if listed previously:

Describe:

_____

_____

Owner:_____

Value .... $ _____

Describe:

_____

_____

Owner:_____

Value .... $ _____

Was any of your property or your spouse's received by gift or inheritance? _____

If YES, list all specific property received by gift or inheritance that is still owned (note who owns each item and its value). List property here even if it is listed previously:

Describe:

_____

_____

Owner:_____

Value .... $ _____

Describe:

_____

_____

Owner:_____

Value .... $ _____

Bills and Debts

Credit Cards

Name of company: _____
Reason for debt: _____
In whose name: _____
Monthly payment .... $ _____
Balance due .... $ _____

Name of company: _____
Reason for debt: _____
In whose name: _____
Monthly payment .... $ _____
Balance due .... $ _____

Other Debts

Name of company: _____
Reason for debt: _____
In whose name: _____
Monthly payment .... $ _____
Balance due .... $ _____

Name of company: _____
Reason for debt: _____
In whose name: _____
Monthly payment .... $ _____
Balance due .... $ _____

Name of company: _____
Reason for debt: _____
In whose name: _____
Monthly payment .... $ _____
Balance due .... $ _____

Name of company: _____
Reason for debt: _____
In whose name: _____
Monthly payment .... $ _____
Balance due .... $ _____

Property Division Worksheet

Separate Property

Name of Spouse #1: _____

Description: _____ Value $ _____
Description: _____ Value $ _____
Description: _____ Value $ _____
Description: _____ Value $ _____
Description: _____ Value $ _____
Description: _____ Value $ _____
Description: _____ Value $ _____

Total of Separate Property ....(Spouse #1) $ _____

Name of Spouse #2: _____

Description: _____ Value $ _____
Description: _____ Value $ _____
Description: _____ Value $ _____
Description: _____ Value $ _____
Description: _____ Value $ _____
Description: _____ Value $ _____
Description: _____ Value $ _____

Total of Separate Property ....(Spouse #2) $ _____

Marital Property of Both Spouses

Real estate: _____ Value $ _____
Auto: _____ Value $ _____
Furniture: _____ Value $ _____
Cash: _____ Value $ _____
Jewelry: _____ Value $ _____
Tools: _____ Value $ _____
Other: _____ Value $ _____
Stocks: _____ Value $ _____
Bonds: _____ Value $ _____

Total Amount of Marital Property ....(A) $ _____

Marital Bills and Obligations

Creditor: _____ Balance $ _____
Creditor: _____ Balance $ _____
Creditor: _____ Balance $ _____
Creditor: _____ Balance $ _____
Creditor: _____ Balance $ _____
Creditor: _____ Balance $ _____

Total Amount of Marital Bills ....(B) $ _____

Value of Marital Property to Be Divided

Total Amount of Marital Property .... (A) $ _____
Minus (-) Total Amount of Marital Bills ....(B) $ _____
Equals (=) *Total Value to be Divided* [A - B = C] ....(C) $ _____

Approximate Value to Each Spouse (One-half of C or C÷2) .... $ _____

Agreed Share of Marital Property and Bills for Each Spouse

Name of Spouse #1: _____

Description: _____ Value $ _____
Description: _____ Value $ _____
Description: _____ Value $ _____
Description: _____ Value $ _____
Description: _____ Value $ _____
Description: _____ Value $ _____
Description: _____ Value $ _____
Description: _____ Value $ _____

Total Marital Property ....(Spouse #1) $ _____

Name of Spouse #2: _____

Description: _____ Value $ _____
Description: _____ Value $ _____
Description: _____ Value $ _____
Description: _____ Value $ _____
Description: _____ Value $ _____
Description: _____ Value $ _____
Description: _____ Value $ _____
Description: _____ Value $ _____

Total Marital Property ....(Spouse #2) $ _____

Alimony

The right to alimony in a modern divorce setting is no longer the sole province of the wife. Both spouses are considered to be equally eligible to receive alimony under the laws in all states. Alimony awards are not commonly awarded to either spouse, however. Such awards are made only in approximately 15 percent of all divorces. Spousal support after marriage is definitely not common, and you should approach your discussion of alimony with this fact firmly in mind. In certain situations, however, alimony is an important and valuable right. Please note that the marital settlement agreement in this book provides for *no alimony for either spouse*.

The approach that most courts have taken to making decisions about alimony has been to review a list of factors that are relevant to supporting a spouse. Other than these lists of factors, there have generally been no set guidelines provided to use in determining the actual amount of alimony to award. If you and your spouse cannot reach an agreement regarding alimony, you may need to seek legal assistance in order to protect your rights to sufficient future alimony. In cases where you decide that alimony is not necessary, a lawyer is generally not needed. However, if your marriage has been of long duration and one of you will be reasonably incapable of self-support in the future, it is recommended that you seek the assistance of a competent attorney. In such cases, alimony may be the most important economic factor in the divorce and may be the only method by which a spouse who is not self-sufficient will be able to achieve a secure life. In cases where alimony will be a major factor and will constitute the primary economic support for one spouse, many other factors become important; for example, cost-of-living adjustments and long-term tax consequences. The advice of a lawyer is generally necessary in such situations. Please note that all of the information that is listed on both the Property Questionnaire and Property Division Worksheet found earlier in this chapter is relevant to any discussion of alimony and may be necessary for filling in the Alimony Questionnaire. Please refer to those forms when necessary.

Alimony Questionnaire

Name of Spouse Filling out Form _____

How long have you been married? _____
Are you presently employed? _____
   If YES, where?

_____
_____

   For how long? _____
   What rate of pay? $ _____
   What education was necessary? _____
Prior to that what was your former job? _____
   Where?

_____
_____

   For how long? _____
   What rate of pay? $ _____
   What education was necessary? _____
Prior to that what was your former job? _____
   Where?

_____
_____

   For how long? _____
   What rate of pay? $ _____
   What education was necessary? _____
If you are not now employed, when was your last job? _____
   Where?

_____
_____

   For how long? _____
   What rate of pay? $ _____
   What education was necessary? _____
Were you employed at the time of your marriage? _____
   If YES, where?

_____
_____

   For how long? _____
   What rate of pay? $ _____
   What education was necessary? _____

What was the level of education that you had attained at the time of your marriage? _____

_____

What level of education have you attained now? _____

What job skills, training, or experience did you have at the time of your marriage? _____

_____

_____

_____

_____

What job skills, training, or experience do you now have? _____

_____

_____

_____

_____

What is your usual occupation? _____

What will be your monthly income at the time of your separation?

$ _____

What will be your monthly expenses at the time of your separation?

$ _____

What will be the value of your property at the time of your separation?

$ _____

How long would it take you to achieve the education or skills necessary to be able to individually attain the standard of living that you enjoyed during your marriage? _____

_____

At any time during your marriage, did your spouse attend college or a special or professional training course? _____

Did you sacrifice any career opportunities in order to allow your spouse to attend school or achieve success in his or her occupation? _____

Do you feel that you will be able to be self-sufficient after your divorce? _____

_____

Do you anticipate any unusual expenses or circumstances in the near future which may affect your ability to become self-supporting? _____

_____

_____

Do you and your spouse have any type of written premarital agreement? _____

If YES, what are the details that relate to alimony? _____

_____

_____

Do you feel that you deserve alimony? _____

If YES, how much? $ _____

Should it be paid in a lump-sum? _____

Should it be paid in monthly payments? _____

If YES, how long should the payments continue? _____

Preparing and Signing Your Marital Settlement Agreement

1. As you prepare the Marital Settlement Agreement, you should have before you all of the questionnaires and worksheet from this chapter that you have completed. Make a photocopy of the entire agreement as provided in this book or use the form on the Forms-on-CD. Fill in the names, addresses, and marital information as called for in the first two paragraphs of the document.

2. Using your Property Division Worksheet, fill in the description of the property that is to be the wife's, free and clear. Then fill in the property that is to be the husband's. After this, fill in the bills or debts that the wife is to pay and those which the husband is to pay.

3. Decide who is to get the tax refund for the current year and who will pay any of the taxes due. If the wife desires to be known by her former name, insert that name in the appropriate blank. Finally, insert the name of the state in which you are living, or if living in separate states, the name of the state in which you lived as a married couple.

4. There are various other marital settlement agreement issues that are included in order for your agreement to have the necessary legal force. These standard legal phrases are important and should not be altered. They cover the following points:

    *   That you both want the terms of your marital settlement agreement to be the basis for a court order in the event of a divorce
    *   That you both have prepared complete and honest Financial Statements and that they are attached to your agreement
    *   That you both know you have the right to see your own lawyers and that you both understand your legal rights
    *   That you both will sign any necessary documents
    *   That you both intend for your agreement to be the full statement of your rights and responsibilities
    *   That your agreement will be binding on any future representatives of yours (such as an executor of your estate, should you die)

5. Finally, the entire document should be retyped (or printed from the enclosed Forms-on-CD) on clean letter-sized paper and both spouses should sign the agreement in the presence of a notary public and two witnesses (who can be any unrelated persons).

Marital Settlement Agreement

This agreement is made on _____ , between
_____ , the Wife,
address:

and _____ , the Husband,
address:

We were married on _____ , County of
_____ , State of _____ .

As a result of disputes and serious difficulties, we sincerely believe that our marriage is irretrievably broken and that there is no possible chance for reconciliation. As a result of irreconcilable disputes and serious differences, we have separated and are now living apart and intend to continue to remain permanently apart. We both desire to settle by agreement all of our marital affairs, including the division of all of our property and bills, and our rights to alimony, spousal support, or maintenance.

We both desire to settle by agreement all of our marital affairs,
THEREFORE, in consideration of our mutual promises, and other good and valuable consideration, we agree as follows:

We both desire and agree to permanently live separate and apart from each other, as if we were single, according to the terms of this agreement. We each agree not to annoy, harass, or interfere with the other in any manner.

We both agree that we will cooperate in the filing of any necessary tax returns. We also agree that any tax refunds for the current year will be the property of the _____ and that any taxes due for the current tax year will be paid by the _____ .

We both agree that, in the event of divorce or dissolution of marriage, the _____ desires to and shall have the right to be known by the name of

_____

Page ____ of ____ pages   Husband's initials _____   Wife's initials _____

148

Division of Property

To settle all issues relating to our property, we both agree that the following property shall be the sole and separate property of the Wife, and the Husband transfers and quitclaims any interest that he may have in this property to the Wife:

We also agree that the following property shall be the sole and separate property of the Husband, and the Wife transfers and quitclaims any interest that she may have in this property to the Husband:

Division of Bills

To settle all issues relating to our debts, we agree that the Wife shall pay and indemnify and hold the Husband harmless from the following debts:

We agree that the Husband shall pay and indemnify and hold the Wife harmless from the following debts:

We also agree not to incur any further debts or obligations for which the other may be liable.

Page _____ of _____ pages   Husband's initials _____   Wife's initials _____

Alimony

To settle any and all issues regarding alimony and maintenance, we both agree that:

Additional Terms

We further agree to the following additional terms:

Signature

We each understand that we have the right to representation by separate lawyers. We each fully understand our rights and we each consider the terms of this agreement to be fair and reasonable. Both of us agree to execute and deliver any documents, make any endorsements, and do any and all acts that may be necessary or convenient to carry out all of the terms of this agreement.

We agree that this document is intended to be the full and entire settlement and agreement between us regarding our marital rights and obligations and that this agreement should be interpreted and governed by the laws of the State of _____ .

We also agree that every provision of this agreement is expressly made binding upon the heirs, assigns, executors, administrators, successors in interest, and representatives of each of us.

We both desire that, in the event of our divorce or dissolution of marriage, this marital settlement agreement be approved and merged and incorporated into any subsequent decree or judgment for divorce or dissolution of marriage and that, by the terms of the judgment or decree, we both be ordered to comply with the terms of this agreement, but that this agreement shall survive.

Page _____ of _____ pages   Husband's initials _____   Wife's initials _____

We have prepared this agreement cooperatively and each of us has fully and honestly disclosed to the other the extent of our assets, income, and financial situation. We have each completed Financial Statements that are attached to this agreement and are incorporated by reference.

Signed and dated this day _____ , 20 _____

_____   _____
Signature of Wife   Signature of Husband

_____   _____
Printed Name of Wife   Printed Name of Husband

_____   _____
Signature of Witness #1   Signature of Witness #2

_____   _____
Printed Name of Witness #1   Printed Name of Witness #2

_____   _____
Address of Witness #1   Address of Witness #2

Notary Acknowledgment

State of _____
County of _____

On _____ , 20 _____ , _____ ,
and _____ , husband and wife, and
_____ and _____ , their
witnesses, personally came before me and, being duly sworn, did state that they are the persons described in the above document and that they signed the above document in my presence as a free and voluntary act for the purposes stated.

_____
Signature of Notary Public

Notary Public, In and for the County of _____
State of _____

My commission expires: _____   Notary Seal

Page _____ of _____ pages   Husband's initials _____   Wife's initials _____

Financial Statement Instructions

The following Financial Statement will be your record of the disclosures that you and your spouse have made to each other regarding your joint and individual economic situations. The statement details both your monthly income and expenses and your overall *net worth* (assets and liabilities). The information that you include on this form should be current and should be based upon your economic situation immediately *after* your marital settlement agreement takes effect. The monthly income that you list should be based on your current job and sources of income. The expenses that you include on this statement should be based on your estimated or actual expenses while you are living separately from your spouse. The assets and liabilities listed should be your separate and marital property and bills that you and your spouse have agreed to divide in your Marital Settlement Agreement. Fill in only those items that apply to your circumstances.

Each of your Financial Statements will become a permanent part of your Marital Settlement Agreement. Both you and your spouse will need to prepare an individual copy of this statement. This form assures that both you and your spouse are fully aware of each other's economic circumstances and that you have made your decisions and agreements based on having full knowledge of all of the facts relating to your property and income.

Once both of you have filled in the appropriate blanks on the following form or on the form on the CD, retype the entire document on clean white letter-sized paper. Then sign the document before a notary public and attach both Financial Statements to your Marital Settlement Agreement.

Financial Statement of _____

Employment

Occupation: _____
Employed by: _____
Address of Employer: _____
Pay period: _____
Next pay day: _____
Rate of pay .... $ _____

Average Monthly Income

Gross monthly salary or wages .... $ _____
   Deductions from paycheck on monthly basis
      Social Security .... $ _____
      Income tax .... $ _____
      Insurance .... $ _____
      Credit Union .... $ _____
      Union dues .... $ _____
      Other deductions .... $ _____
     Total Deductions .... $ _____
Net monthly salary or wages (gross minus [-] total deductions) .... $ _____

Monthly income from other sources
      Commissions, bonuses, etc. .... $ _____
      Unemployment, welfare, etc. .... $ _____
      Dividends, interest, etc. .... $ _____
      Business income .... $ _____
      Rents, royalties .... $ _____
      Other monthly income .... $ _____
Net monthly income from other sources.. $ _____

Total Average Monthly Income .... (A) $ _____

Average Monthly Expenses

Mortgage or rental payment .... $ _____
Property taxes .... $ _____
Homeowner's insurance .... $ _____
Electricity .... $ _____
Water, garbage, sewer .... $ _____
Cable television .... $ _____
Telephone .... $ _____
Fuel oil and natural gas .... $ _____
Cleaning and laundry .... $ _____

Repairs and maintenance .... $ _____

Pest control .... $ _____

Housewares .... $ _____

Food and grocery items .... $ _____

Meals outside home .... $ _____

Clothing .... $ _____

Medical, dental, prescriptions .... $ _____

Education .... $ _____

Childcare/babysitter .... $ _____

Entertainment .... $ _____

Gifts or donations .... $ _____

Vacation expenses .... $ _____

Public transportation .... $ _____

Automobile

    Gasoline and oil .... $ _____

    Repairs .... $ _____

    License .... $ _____

    Insurance .... $ _____

    Payments .... $_____

Insurance

    Health .... $ _____

    Disability .... $ _____

    Life .... $ _____

    Other .... $ _____

Any other expenses (list)

    _____ $ _____

    _____ $ _____

Fixed debts on a monthly basis

    Creditor _____ Monthly payment $ _____

    Creditor _____ Monthly payment $ _____

Any other debts

    Creditor _____ Monthly payment $ _____

    Creditor _____ Monthly payment $ _____

Total Average Monthly Expenses .... (B) $ _____

Assets

Cash .... $ _____

Stocks .... $ _____

Bonds .... $ _____

Real estate .... $ _____

Automobiles .... $ _____

Contents of home or apartment .... $ _____

Jewelry .... $ _____

Any other assets (list)

_____ $ _____

_____ $ _____

Total Assets .... (C) $ _____

Liabilities

Creditor _____ Total balance due $ _____

Creditor _____ Total balance due $ _____

Total Liabilities .... (D) $ _____

Summary of Income and Expenses

Total Average Monthly Income .... (A) $ _____

Total Average Monthly Expenses .... (B) $ _____

Summary Of Assets And Liabilities

Total Assets .... (C) $ _____

Total Liabilities .... (D) $ _____

Signed and dated this day _____ , 20 _____

_____   _____

Signature   Printed Name

State of _____

County of _____

On _____ , 20 _____ , before me, the undersigned authority, in and for and residing in the above county and state, personally appeared _____ , who is personally known to me to be the same person whose name is subscribed to the foregoing document, and, being duly sworn, verified that the information contained in the foregoing document is true and correct on personal knowledge and acknowledged that said document was signed as a free and voluntary act.

_____

Signature of Notary Public

Notary Public, In and for the County of _____

State of _____

My commission expires: _____   Notary Seal

CHAPTER 10
Releases

A release is a method of acknowledging the satisfaction of an obligation or of releasing parties from liability or claims. Releases are used in various situations: from releasing a person or company from liability after an accident, to a release of liens or claims against property. They can be a useful means of settling minor disputes. One party may pay another to release a claim. For example: Andy pays Bill $200.00 to release Bill's claims for damages incurred when Andy's truck damaged Bill's garage.

Releases can be very powerful documents. The various releases contained in this chapter are tailored to meet the most common situations in which a release is used. For a release to be valid, there must be some type of *consideration* (a promise to do or not do something) received by the person who is granting the release. The specific details of the particular consideration need not be specified in a release. Releases should be used carefully as they may prevent any future claims against the party to whom they are granted. In general, a release from claims relating to an accident that causes personal injury should not be signed without a prior examination by a doctor. Also note that a release relating to damage to community property in a "community property" state must be signed by both spouses. Study the various forms provided in this chapter to determine which one is proper for the use intended. Please note that Chapter 16: *Personal Loan Documents* contains a Release of Security Interest and a Release of U.C.C. (Uniform Commercial Code) Financing Statement and Chapter 17: *Promissory Notes* contains a Release of Promissory Note. Please refer to those chapters for explanations of those particular release forms. *Note*: If you are at all unsure of the correct use of any forms in this chapter, please consult a competent attorney. The following releases are included in this chapter:

General Release: This release serves as a full blanket release of obligations from one party to another. It should only be used when all obligations of one party are to be released. The party signing this release is discharging the other party from all of their obligations to the signing party stemming from a specific incident or transaction. This form can be used when one party has a claim against a second party and the second agrees to waive the claim for payment.

Mutual Release: The mutual release form provides a method for two parties to jointly release each other from their mutual obligations or claims. This form should be used when both parties intend to discharge each other from all of their mutual obligations. It essentially serves the purpose of two mutual and reciprocal General Releases between two separate parties.

Specific Release: This release form should be used when only a particular claim or obligation is being released, while allowing other liabilities to continue. The obligation being released should be spelled out in careful and precise terms to prevent confusion with any other obligation or claim. In addition, the liabilities that are not being released but will survive, should also be carefully noted.

General Release

For consideration, I, _____ ,
address:

release _____ ,
address:

from all claims and obligations, known or unknown, to this date arising from the following transaction or incident:

The party signing this release has not assigned any claims or obligations covered by this release to any other party.

The party signing this release intends that it both bind and benefit itself and any successors.

Dated _____ , 20 _____

_____
Signature

_____
Printed Name

Mutual Release

For consideration, _____ ,
address:

and _____ ,
address:

release each other from all claims and obligations, known or unknown, that they may have against each other arising from the following transaction or incident:

Neither party has assigned any claims or obligations covered by this release to any other party.

Both parties signing this release intend that it both bind and benefit themselves and any successors.

Dated _____ , 20 _____

_____   _____
Signature   Signature

_____   _____
Printed Name   Printed Name

Specific Release

For consideration, I, _____ ,
address:

release _____ ,
address:

from the following specific claims and obligations:

arising from the following transaction or incident:

Any claims or obligations that are not specifically mentioned are not released by this Specific Release.

The party signing this release has not assigned any claims or obligations covered by this release to any other party.

The party signing this release intends that it both bind and benefit itself and any successors.

Dated _____ , 20 _____

_____
Signature

_____
Printed Name

CHAPTER 11

Receipts

In this chapter, various receipt forms are provided. In general, receipts are a formal acknowledgment of having received something, whether it is money or property. These forms do not have to be notarized. Please note that Chapter 12: *Leases of Real Estate* contains a Receipt for Lease Security Deposit and a Rent Receipt to be used in conjunction with leases of real estate. The following receipt forms are included in this chapter:

Receipt in Full: This form should be used as a receipt for a payment that completely pays off a debt. You will need to include the amount paid, the name of the person who paid it, the date when paid, and a description of the obligation that is paid off (for example: an invoice, statement, or bill of sale). The original receipt should go to the person making the payment, but a copy should be retained.

Receipt on Account: This form should be used as a receipt for a payment that does not fully pay off a debt, but, rather, is a payment on account and is credited to the total balance due. You will need to include the amount paid, the name of the person who paid it, the date when paid, and a description of the account to which the payment is to be applied. The original receipt should go to the person making the payment, but a copy should be kept by you.

Receipt for Goods: This form should be used as a receipt for the acceptance of goods. It is intended to be used in conjunction with a delivery order or purchase order. It also states that the goods have been inspected and found to be in conformance with the order. The original of this receipt should be retained by the person delivering the goods and a copy should go to the person accepting delivery.

Note: If you are at all unsure of the correct use of any forms in this chapter, please consult a competent attorney.

Receipt in Full

The undersigned acknowledges receipt of the sum of $ _____ paid by
_____ .

This payment constitutes full payment and satisfaction of the following obligation:

Dated _____ , 20 _____

_____
Signature of Person Receiving Payment

_____
Printed Name of Person Receiving Payment

Receipt on Account

The undersigned acknowledges receipt of the sum of $ _____ paid by
_____ .

This payment will be applied and credited to the following account:

Dated _____ , 20 _____

_____
Signature of Person Receiving Payment

_____
Printed Name of Person Receiving Payment

Receipt for Goods

The undersigned acknowledges receipt of the goods which are described on the attached purchase order. The undersigned also acknowledges that these goods have been inspected and found to be in conformance with the purchase order specifications.

Dated _____ , 20 _____

_____
Signature of Person Receiving Goods

_____
Printed Name of Person Receiving Goods

CHAPTER 12
Leases of Real Estate

A *lease* of real estate is simply a written contract for one party to rent a specific property from another for a certain amount and for a certain time period. As such, all of the general legal ramifications that relate to contracts also relate to leases. However, all states have additional requirements which pertain only to leases. If the rental period is to be for one year or more, most states require that leases be in writing. Leases can be prepared for *periodic* tenancies (that is, for example, month-to-month or week-to-week) or they can be for a *fixed* period (for example, from one specific date to another specific date). The lease contained in this chapter provides for a fixed-period tenancy.

There are also general guidelines for security deposits in most states. These most often follow a reasonable pattern and should be adhered to. Most states provide for the following with regard to lease security deposits:

- Security deposits should be no greater than one month's rent and should be fully refundable
- Security deposits should be used for the repair of damages only and not applied for the nonpayment of rent (an additional month's rent may be requested to cover potential nonpayment of rent situations)
- Security deposits should be kept in a separate, interest-bearing account and returned, with interest, to the tenant within 10 days of termination of a lease (minus, of course, any deductions for damages)

In addition to state laws regarding security deposits, many states have requirements relating to the time periods required prior to terminating a lease. These rules have evolved over time to prevent both the landlord or the tenant from being harmed by early termination of a lease. In general, if the lease is for a fixed time period, the termination of the lease is governed by the lease itself. Early termination of a fixed-period lease may, however, be governed by individual state law. For periodic leases (month-to-month, etc.), there are normally state rules as to how much advance notice must be given prior to the termination of a lease. If early lease termination is anticipated, state law regarding this issue should be checked. A good site to check state laws online is www.cornell.edu/topics/state_statutes.html

The following forms are included in this chapter:

Residential Lease: This form should be used when renting a residential property. The following information will be necessary to prepare this form:

- The name and address of the landlord
- The name and address of the tenant
- A complete legal description of the leased property
- The length of time the lease will be in effect
- The amount of the rental payments
- The day of the month when the rent will be due
- The due date of the first rent payment
- The amount of the security deposit for damages
- The amount of additional rent held as rental default deposit
- Any utilities that the landlord will supply
- The utilities that the tenant will provide
- Any other additional terms; for example, no pets

Although the landlord and tenant can agree to any terms they desire, this particular lease provides for the following basic terms to be included:

- A fixed period term for the lease
- A security deposit for damages that will be returned within 10 days after the termination of the lease
- An additional month's rent as security for payment of the rent that will be returned within 10 days after the termination of the lease
- The tenant's agreement to keep the property in good repair and not make any alterations without consent
- The tenant's agreement not to assign the lease or sublet the property without the landlord's consent
- The landlord's right to inspect the property on a reasonable basis and that the tenant has already inspected it and found the property satisfactory
- The landlord's right to reenter and take possession upon breach of the lease (as long as it is in accordance with state law)
- Any other additional terms that the parties agree upon

Assignment of Lease: This form is for use if one party to a lease is assigning its full interest in the lease to another party. This effectively substitutes one party for another under a lease. This particular assignment form has both of the parties agreeing to indemnify and hold each other harmless for any failures to perform under the lease while they were the party liable under it. This *indemnify and hold harmless* clause simply means that if a claim arises for failure to perform, each party agrees to be responsible for the period of their own performance obligations. A description of the lease that is assigned should include the parties to the lease, a description of the property, and the date of the lease. Other information that is necessary to complete the assignment of lease is the name and address of the *assignor* (the party who is assigning the lease), the name and address of the *assignee* (the party to whom the lease is being assigned), and the date of the assignment. A copy of the original lease should be attached to this form. A copy of a Consent to Assignment of Lease should also be attached, if necessary.

Consent to Assignment of Lease: This form is used if the original lease states that the consent of the landlord is necessary for the assignment of the lease to be valid. A description of the lease and the name and signature of the person giving the consent are all that is necessary for completing this form. A copy of the original lease should be attached to this form.

Notice of Assignment of Lease: If a third party is involved in any of the obligations or benefits of an assigned lease, that party should be notified of the assignment in writing. This alerts the third party to look to the new party for satisfaction of any obligations under the lease or to make any payments under the lease directly to the new party. Information necessary to complete this form are the names and addresses of the parties to the lease, a description of the lease, and the effective date of the assignment of the lease. A copy of the original lease should be attached to this form. A copy of a Consent to Assignment of Lease should also be attached, if necessary.

Amendment of Lease: Use this form to modify any terms of a lease (except for the expiration date, which is explained under "Extension of Lease" below). This amendment may be used to change any portion of the lease. Simply note what changes are being made in the appropriate place on this form. If a portion of the lease is being deleted, make note of the deletion. If certain language is being substituted, state the substitution clearly. If additional language is being added, make this clear. For example, you may wish to use language as follows:

- "Paragraph _____ is deleted from this lease"
- "Paragraph _____ is deleted from this lease and the following paragraph is substituted in its place:"
- "The following new paragraph is added to this lease:"

A copy of the original lease should be attached to this form.

Extension of Lease: This document should be used to extend the effective time period during which a lease is in force. The use of this form allows the time limit to be extended without having to entirely redraft the lease. Under this document, all of the other terms of the lease will remain the same, with only the expiration date changing. You will need to fill in the original expiration date and the new expiration date. Other information necessary will be the names and addresses of the parties to the lease and a description of the lease. A copy of the original lease should be attached to this form.

Sublease: This form is used if the tenant subleases property covered by an original lease. This particular sublease form has both of the parties agreeing to indemnify and hold each other harmless for any failures to perform under the lease while they were the party liable under it. This indemnify and hold harmless clause simply means that if a claim arises for failure to perform, each party agrees to be responsible for the period of their own performance obligations. A description of the lease that is subleased should include the parties to the lease, a description of the property, and the date of the lease. Other information that is necessary to complete the sublease are the name and address of the original tenant, the name and address of the *subtenant* (the party to whom the property is being subleased), and the date of the sublease. A copy of the original lease should be attached to this form. A copy of a Consent to Sublease of Lease should also be attached, if necessary.

Consent to Sublease of Lease: This form is used if the original lease states that the consent of the landlord is necessary for a sublease to be valid. A description of the lease and the name and signature of the person giving the consent are all that is necessary for completing this form. A copy of the original lease should be attached to this form.

Notice of Breach of Lease: This form should be used to notify a party to a lease of the violation of a term of the lease or of an instance of failure to perform a required duty under the lease. It provides for a description of the alleged violation of the lease and for a time period in which the party is instructed to cure the breach of the lease. If the breach is not taken care of within the time period allowed, a lawyer should be consulted for further action, which may entail a lawsuit to enforce the lease terms. A copy of the original lease should be attached to this form.

Notice of Rent Default: This form allows for notice to a tenant of default in the payment of rent. It provides for the amount of the defaulted payments to be specified and for a time limit to be placed on payment before further action is taken. If the breach is not taken care of within the time period allowed, a lawyer should be consulted for further action, which may involve a lawsuit to enforce the lease terms. A copy of the original lease should be attached to this form.

Notice to Vacate Property: This notice informs a tenant who has already been notified of a breach of the lease (or of a late rent payment) to vacate the property. It sets a specific date by which the tenant must be out of the property. If the tenant fails to leave by the date set, an attorney should be consulted to begin eviction efforts.

Landlord's Notice to Terminate Lease: By this notice, a landlord may inform a tenant of the landlord's termination of a lease for breach of the lease. This action may be taken under the leases provided in this book because there are specific lease provisions that allow this action and (presumably) the tenant has agreed to these provisions. To complete this form, the lease should be described, the breach of the lease should be described, the date of the original Notice of Breach of Lease should be noted, and a date on which the tenant should deliver possession of the property to the landlord should be set.

Tenant's Notice to Terminate Lease: By this notice, a tenant may inform a landlord of the tenant's termination of a lease for breach of the lease. This action may be taken under the leases provided in this book because there are specific lease provisions that allow this action and (presumably) the landlord has agreed to these provisions. To complete this form, the lease should be described, the breach of the lease (reason for termination) should be described, and the date for delivery of possession back to the landlord should be set.

Mutual Termination of Lease: This form should be used when both the landlord and tenant desire to terminate a lease. To complete, simply fill in the names of the landlord and tenant and a description of the lease. This document releases both parties from any claims that one party may have against the other for any actions under the lease. It also states that the landlord agrees that the rent has been paid in full and that the property has been delivered in good condition.

Receipt for Lease Security Deposit: This form is to be used for receipt of a lease security deposit. The amount of the deposit and a description of the leased property are all that is necessary for completion.

Rent Receipt: This form may be used as a receipt for the periodic payment of rent. It provides for the amount paid, the period paid for, and a description of the property.

Notice of Lease: This document should be used to record notice that a parcel of real estate has a current lease in effect on it. This may be necessary if the property is on the market for sale or may be required by a bank or mortgage company. Requiring a notarization, this form may be completed with the following information: name and address of the landlord and tenant, description of the property, term of the lease, and any options to extend.

Note: If you are at all unsure of the correct use of any forms in this chapter, please consult a competent attorney.

Residential Lease

This Residential Lease is made on _____ , 20 _____ , between
_____ , Landlord,
address:

and _____ , Tenant,
address:

1. The Landlord agrees to rent to the Tenant and the Tenant agrees to rent from the Landlord the following residence:

2. The term of this lease will be from _____ , 20 _____ , until _____ , 20 _____ .

3. The rental payments will be $ _____ per _____ and will be payable by the Tenant to the Landlord on the _____ day of each month, beginning on _____ , 20 _____ .

4. The Tenant has paid the Landlord a security deposit of $ _____ . This security deposit will be held as security for the repair of any damages to the residence by the Tenant. This deposit will be returned to the Tenant within ten (10) days of the termination of this lease, minus any amounts needed to repair the residence.

5. The Tenant has paid the Landlord an additional month's rent in the amount of $ _____ . This rent deposit will be held as security for the payment of rent by the Tenant. This rent payment deposit will be returned to the Tenant within ten (10) days of the termination of this lease, minus any rent still due upon termination.

6. The Tenant agrees to maintain the residence in a clean and sanitary manner and not to make any alterations to the residence without the Landlord's written consent. Tenant also agrees not to conduct any business in the residence. At the termination of this lease, the Tenant agrees to leave the residence in the same condition as when it was received, except for normal wear and tear.

7. The Landlord agrees to supply the following utilities to the Tenant:

8. The Tenant agrees to obtain and pay for the following utilities:

9. Tenant agrees not to sublet the residence or assign this lease without the Landlord's written consent. Tenant agrees to allow the Landlord reasonable access to the residence for inspection and repair. Landlord agrees to enter the residence only after notifying the Tenant in advance, except in an emergency.

10. The Tenant has inspected the residence and has found it satisfactory.

11. If the Tenant fails to pay the rent on time or violates any other terms of this lease, the Landlord will have the right to terminate this lease in accordance with state law. The Landlord will also have the right to re-enter the residence and take possession of it and to take advantage of any other legal remedies available.

12. The following are additional terms of this lease:

13. The parties agree that this lease is the entire agreement between them. This lease binds and benefits both the Landlord and Tenant and any successors.

_____   _____
Signature of Landlord   Signature of Tenant

_____   _____
Printed Name of Landlord   Printed Name of Tenant

Assignment of Lease

This Assignment of Lease is made on _____ , 20 _____ , between
_____ , Assignor,
address:

and _____ , Assignee,
address:

For valuable consideration, the parties agree to the following terms and conditions:

1. The Assignor assigns all interest, burdens, and benefits in the following described lease
    to the Assignee:

    This lease is attached to this assignment and is a part of this assignment.

2. The Assignor warrants that this lease is in effect, has not been modified, and is fully as-
    signable. If the consent of the Landlord is necessary for this assignment to be effective,
    such consent is attached to this assignment and is a part of this assignment. Assignor agrees
    to indemnify and hold the Assignee harmless from any claim which may result from the
    Assignor's failure to perform under this lease prior to the date of this assignment.

3. The Assignee agrees to perform all of the obligations of the Assignor and receive all of
    the benefits of the Assignor under this lease. Assignee agrees to indemnify and hold the
    Assignor harmless from any claim which may result from the Assignee's failure to per-
    form under this lease after the date of this assignment.

4. This assignment binds and benefits both parties and any successors. This document,
    including any attachments, is the entire agreement between the parties.

_____   _____
Signature of Assignor   Signature of Assignee

_____   _____
Printed Name of Assignor   Printed Name of Assignee

Consent to Assignment of Lease

Date: _____ , 20 _____

To:_____

I am the Landlord under the following described lease:

This lease is the subject of the attached Assignment of Lease.

I consent to the assignment of this lease as described in the attached assignment, which provides that the Assignee is fully substituted for the Assignor.

_____
Signature of Landlord

_____
Printed Name of Landlord

Notice of Assignment of Lease

Date: _____ , 20 _____

To: _____

RE: Assignment of Lease

Dear _____ :

This notice is in reference to the following described lease:

Please be advised that as of _____ , 20 _____ , all interest and rights under this lease which were formerly owned by

_____ , Assignor

address:

have been permanently assigned to

_____ , Assignee

address:

Please be advised that all of the obligations and rights of the former party to this lease are now the responsibility of the new party to this lease.

_____

Signature of Assignor

_____

Printed Name of Assignor

Amendment of Lease

This Amendment of Lease is made on _____ , 20 ____ , between

_____ , Landlord,

address:

and _____ , Tenant,

address:

For valuable consideration, the parties agree as follows:

1. The following described lease is attached to this amendment and is made a part of this amendment:

2. The parties agree to amend this lease as follows:

3. All other terms and conditions of the original lease remain in effect without modification. This amendment binds and benefits both parties and any successors. This document, including the attached lease, is the entire agreement between the parties.

The parties have signed this amendment on the date specified at the beginning of this amendment.

_____   _____
Signature of Landlord   Signature of Tenant

_____   _____
Printed Name of Landlord   Printed Name of Tenant

Extension of Lease

This Extension of Lease is made on _____ , 20 ____ , between
_____ , Landlord,
address:

and _____ , Tenant,
address:

For valuable consideration, the parties agree as follows:

1. The following described lease will end on _____ , 20 ____ :

    This lease is attached to this extension and is a part of this extension.

2. The parties agree to extend this lease for an additional period, which will begin
    immediately on the expiration of the original time period and will end on
    _____ , 20 ____ .

3. The extension of this lease will be on the same terms and conditions as the original lease.
    This extension binds and benefits both parties and any successors. This document, including the attached lease, is the entire agreement between the parties.

The parties have signed this extension on the date specified at the beginning of this extension.

_____   _____
Signature of Landlord   Signature of Tenant

_____   _____
Printed Name of Landlord   Printed Name of Tenant

Sublease

This Sublease is made on _____ , 20 _____ , between
_____ , Tenant,
address:

and _____ , Subtenant,
address:

For valuable consideration, the parties agree to the following terms and conditions:

1. The Tenant subleases to the Subtenant the following described property:

2. This property is currently leased to the Tenant under the terms of the following described lease:

    This lease is attached to this sublease and is a part of this sublease.

3. This sublease will be for the period from _____ , 20 _____ ,
    to _____ , 20 _____ .

4. The subrental payments will be $ _____ per _____ and will be payable by
    the Subtenant to the Landlord on the _____ day of each month, beginning
    on _____ , 20 _____ .

5. The Tenant warrants that the underlying lease is in effect, has not been modified, and that the property may be sublet. If the consent of the Landlord is necessary for this sublease to be effective, such consent is attached to this sublease and is a part of this sublease. Tenant agrees to indemnify and hold the Subtenant harmless from any claim which may result from the Tenant's failure to perform under this lease prior to the date of this sublease.

6. The Subtenant agrees to perform all of the obligations of the Tenant under the original lease and receive all of the benefits of the Tenant under this lease. Subtenant agrees to indemnify and hold the Tenant harmless from any claim which may result from the Subtenant's failure to perform under this lease after the date of this sublease.

7. The Tenant agrees to remain primarily liable to the Landlord for the obligations under the lease.

8. The parties agree to the following additional terms:

9. This sublease binds and benefits both parties and any successors. This sublease, including any attachments, is the entire agreement between the parties.

_____   _____
Signature of Tenant   Signature of Subtenant

_____   _____
Printed Name of Tenant   Printed Name of Subtenant

Consent to Sublease of Lease

Date: _____ , 20 _____

To: _____

I am the Landlord under the following described lease:

This lease is the subject of the attached sublease.

I consent to the sublease of this lease as described in the attached sublease, which provides that the Subtenant is substituted for the Tenant for the period indicated in the sublease. This consent does not release the Tenant from any obligations under the lease and the Tenant remains fully bound under the lease.

_____
Signature of Landlord

_____
Printed Name of Landlord

178

Notice of Breach of Lease

Date: _____ , 20 _____

To: _____

RE: Breach of Lease

Dear _____ :

This notice is in reference to the following described lease:

Please be advised that as of _____ , 20 _____ , we are holding you in BREACH OF LEASE for the following reasons:

If this breach of lease is not corrected within _____ days of this notice, we will take further action to protect our rights, which may include termination of this lease. This notice is made under all applicable laws. All of our rights are reserved under this notice.

_____
Signature of Landlord

_____
Printed Name of Landlord

Notice of Rent Default

Date: _____ , 20 _____

To: _____

RE: Rent Default

Dear _____ :

This notice is in reference to the following described lease:

Please be advised that as of _____ , 20 _____ , you are in DEFAULT IN YOUR PAYMENT OF RENT in the amount of $ _____ .

If this breach of lease is not corrected within _____ days of this notice, we will take further action to protect our rights, which may include termination of this lease and collection proceedings. This notice is made under all applicable laws. All of our rights are reserved under this notice.

_____
Signature of Landlord

_____
Printed Name of Landlord

Notice to Vacate Property

Date: _____ , 20 _____

To: _____

RE: Vacate Property

Dear _____ :

This notice is in reference to the following described lease:

Please be advised that since _____ , 20 _____ , you have been in BREACH OF LEASE for the following reasons:

You were previously notified of this breach in the NOTICE dated
_____ , 20 _____ . At that time you were given
_____ days to correct the breach of the lease and you have not complied.

THEREFORE, YOU ARE HEREBY GIVEN NOTICE:

To immediately vacate the property and deliver possession to the Landlord on or before _____
_____ , 20 _____ . If you fail to correct the breach of lease or vacate
the property by this date, legal action to evict you from the property will be taken. Regardless
of your vacating the property, you are still responsible for all rent due under the lease.

_____
Signature of Landlord

_____
Printed Name of Landlord

Landlord's Notice to Terminate Lease

Date: _____ , 20 _____

To: _____

RE: Terminate Lease

Dear _____ :

This notice is in reference to the following described lease:

Please be advised that as of _____ , 20 _____ , you have been in BREACH OF LEASE for the following reasons:

You were previously notified of this breach in the NOTICE dated _____ , 20 _____ . At that time you were given _____ days to correct the breach of the lease and you have not complied.

THEREFORE, YOU ARE HEREBY GIVEN NOTICE:

The lease is immediately terminated and you are directed to deliver possession of the property to the Landlord on or before _____ , 20 _____ . If you fail to deliver the property by this date, legal action to evict you from the property will be taken. Regardless of your deliverance of the property, you are still responsible for all rent due under the lease.

_____
Signature of Landlord

_____
Printed Name of Landlord

Tenant's Notice to Terminate Lease

Date: _____ , 20 _____

To: _____

RE: Terminate Property

Dear _____ :

This notice is in reference to the following described lease:

Please be advised that as of _____ , 20 _____ , we are terminating the lease for the following reasons:

We intend to deliver possession of the property to the Landlord on or before _____ , 20 _____ .

_____
Signature of Tenant

_____
Printed Name of Tenant

Mutual Termination of Lease

This Termination of Lease is made on _____ , 20 _____ , between
_____ , Landlord,
address:

and _____ , Tenant,
address:

For valuable consideration, the parties agree as follows:

1. The parties are currently bound under the terms of the following described lease:

2. They agree to mutually terminate and cancel this lease effective on this date. This termination agreement will act as a mutual release of all obligations under this lease for both parties, as if the lease has not been entered into in the first place. Landlord agrees that all rent due has been paid and that the possession of the property has been returned in satisfactory condition.

3. This termination binds and benefits both parties and any successors. This document, including the attached lease being terminated, is the entire agreement between the parties.

The parties have signed this termination on the date specified at the beginning of this termination.

_____   _____
Signature of Landlord   Signature of Tenant

_____   _____
Printed Name of Landlord   Printed Name of Tenant

Receipt for Lease Security Deposit

The Landlord acknowledges receipt of the sum of $ _____ paid by the Tenant under the following described lease:

This security deposit payment will be held by the Landlord under the terms of this lease, and unless required by law, will not bear any interest. This security deposit will be repaid when due under the terms of the lease.

Dated: _____ , 20 _____

_____   _____
Signature of Landlord   Printed Name of Landlord

Rent Receipt

The Landlord acknowledges receipt of the sum of $ _____ paid by
_____ , the Tenant.
This payment will be applied and credited to the rent due for the period of
_____ , 20 _____ , on the following described property:

Dated: _____ , 20 _____

_____   _____
Signature of Landlord   Printed Name of Landlord

Notice of Lease

NOTICE is given of the existence of the following lease:

Name of Landlord _____ ,
address:

Name of Tenant _____ ,
address:

Description of property leased:

Term of lease: From _____ , 20 _____ , to
_____ , 20 _____ .

Any options to extend lease:

_____   _____
Signature of Landlord   Printed Name of Landlord

State of _____
County of _____

On _____ , 20 _____ , _____
personally came before me and, being duly sworn, did state that he or she is the person described
in the above document and that he or she signed the above document in my presence.

_____
Signature of Notary Public

Notary Public, In and for the County of _____
State of _____

My commission expires: _____   Notary Seal

CHAPTER 13

Rental of Personal Property

Leases of personal property are often undertaken for the use of tools, equipment, or property necessary to perform a certain task. Other situations where such an agreement is often used is in the rental of property for recreational purposes. The needs of the parties for a personal property rental agreement depend a great deal on the type of property involved and the value of the property.

The two basic forms that are included in this chapter are somewhat at both ends of the spectrum with regard to rental of personal property. The first form is a very simple rental agreement that can be used for short-term rentals of relatively inexpensive property. The second form is a much more complex form that may be used for rentals of more valuable property. A personally tailored form may be constructed by adding particular clauses from the second form to the first form as the circumstances of a particular business situation dictate. Two termination of rental agreement forms are also included. *Note*: If you are at all unsure of the correct use of any forms in this chapter, please consult a competent attorney.

Personal Property Rental Agreement (Simple): This form is designed to be used in situations involving inexpensive property for short terms. As you will see by comparing these clauses to those present in the next form, this form does not address many of the potential problems that may arise in the rental of personal property. However, this simple agreement does provide a legal basis for an enforceable contract between two parties regarding the rental of personal property.

The information necessary for the preparation of this form are simply the names and addresses of the parties (the *owner* and the *renter*), a description of the property, and the amount and term of the rental.

Personal Property Rental Agreement (Complex): This particular form is a far more detailed version of the basic rental agreement described above. The complex agreement is designed to be used in situations that call for more attention to potential problems relating to the rental. This generally means situations in which the property is more valuable.

This agreement addresses the following areas of concern:

- The inspection of the property by the renter and the renter's agreement to use the property in a careful manner
- A warranty by the owner that the property is safe and in good condition
- An indemnity agreement by the renter for damage to the property
- A disclaimer of liability by the owner
- Provisions for a security deposit to cover damages or late rental payments
- An agreement by the renter not to assign or transfer the property
- Responsibility for insuring the property
- Provisions for mediation and arbitration of disputes

The information necessary for filling in this form is as follows:

- The names and addresses of the parties (the owner and the renter)
- A description of the property
- The amount and term of the rental
- The amount of insurance to be provided by the renter
- Any additional terms the parties desire

Renter's Notice to Terminate Rental Agreement: This form is to be used by the renter to provide the written notice required to terminate the complex personal property rental agreement. Simply fill in the name of the renter and owner, a description of the rental agreement, and the date and reason for the termination.

Owner's Notice to Terminate Rental Agreement: This form is essentially identical to the above form, but is designed to be used by the owner (rather than the renter) to terminate the agreement. Fill in the name of the renter and owner, a description of the rental agreement, and the date and reason for the termination.

Personal Property Rental Agreement
(Simple)

This Agreement is made on _____ , 20 _____ , between
_____ , Owner,
address:

and _____ , Renter,
address:

1. The Owner agrees to rent to the Renter and the Renter agrees to rent from the Owner the following property:

2. The term of this agreement will be from _____ o'clock ____ . m.,
    _____ , 20 _____ , until _____ o'clock ____ . m.,
    _____ , 20 _____ .

3. The rental payments will be $ _____ per _____ and will be payable by the Renter to the Owner as follows:

4. This agreement may be terminated by either party by giving twenty-four (24) hours notice to the other party.

5. The parties agree that this agreement is the entire agreement between them. This agreement binds and benefits both the Owner and Renter and any successors.

_____   _____
Signature of Owner   Signature of Renter

_____   _____
Printed Name of Owner   Printed Name of Renter

Personal Property Rental Agreement (Complex)

This Agreement is made on _____ , 20 _____ , between _____ , Owner,
address:

and _____ , Renter,
address:

1. The Owner agrees to rent to the Renter and the Renter agrees to rent from the Owner the following property:

2. The term of this agreement will be from _____ o'clock ____ . m., _____ , 20 _____ , until _____ o'clock ____ . m., _____ , 20 _____ .

3. The rental payments will be $ _____ per _____ and will be payable by the Renter to the Owner as follows:

4. The Renter agrees to pay a late fee of $ _____ per day that the rental payment is late. If the rental payments are in default for over _____ days, the Owner may immediately demand possession of the property without advance notice to the Renter.

5. The Owner warrants that the property is free of any known faults which would affect its safe operation under normal usage and is in good working condition.

6. The Renter states that the property has been inspected and is in good working condition. The Renter agrees to use the property in a safe manner and in normal usage and to maintain the property in good repair. The Renter further agrees not to use the property in a negligent manner or for any illegal purpose.

7. The Renter agrees to fully indemnify the Owner for any damage to or loss of the property during the term of this agreement, unless such loss or damage is caused by a defect of the rented property.

8. The Owner shall not be liable for any injury, loss, or damage caused by any use of the property.

9. The Renter has paid the Owner a security deposit of $ _____ . This security deposit will be held as security for payments of the rent and for the repair of any damages to the property by the Renter. This deposit will be returned to the Renter upon the termination of this agreement, minus any rent still owed to the Owner and minus any amounts needed to repair the property, beyond normal wear and tear.

10. The Renter may not assign or transfer any rights under this agreement to any other person, nor allow the property to be used by any other person, without the written consent of the Owner.

11. Renter agrees to obtain insurance coverage for the property during the term of this rental agreement in the amount of $ _____ . Renter agrees to provide the Owner with a copy of the insurance policy and to not cancel the policy during the term of this rental agreement.

12. This agreement may be terminated by either party by giving twenty-four (24) hours written notice to the other party.

13. Any dispute related to this agreement will be settled by voluntary mediation. If mediation is unsuccessful, the dispute will be settled by binding arbitration using an arbitrator of the American Arbitration Association.

14. The following are additional terms of this agreement:

15. The parties agree that this agreement is the entire agreement between them. This agreement binds and benefits both the Owner and Renter and any successors. Time is of the essence of this agreement.

16. This agreement is governed by the laws of the State of _____ .

_____   _____
Signature of Owner   Signature of Renter

_____   _____
Printed Name of Owner   Printed Name of Renter

Renter's Notice to Terminate Rental Agreement

Date: _____ , 20 _____

To: _____

RE: Notice to Terminate Rental Agreement

Dear _____ :

This notice is in reference to the following described personal property rental agreement:

Please be advised that as of _____ , 20 _____ , we are terminating the personal property rental agreement for the following reasons:

We intend to deliver possession of the property to the Owner on or before _____ , 20 _____ .

_____
Signature of Renter

_____
Printed Name of Renter

Owner's Notice to Terminate Rental Agreement

Date: _____ , 20 _____

To: _____

RE: Notice to Terminate Rental Agreement

Dear _____ :

This notice is in reference to the following described personal property rental agreement:

Please be advised that as of _____ , 20 _____ , we are terminating the personal property rental agreement for the following reasons:

Please deliver possession of the property to the Owner on or before
_____ , 20 _____ .

_____
Signature of Owner

_____
Printed Name of Owner

CHAPTER 14
Sale of Personal Property

The forms in this chapter are for use when selling personal property. A contract for the sale of personal property may be part of a greater transaction (involving, for example, the sale of real estate or a complete business) or it may be prepared separate from any other dealings. A *bill of sale* provides a receipt for both parties that verifies that the sale has been completed and the delivery of the item in question has taken place. Bills of sale are often utilized to document the sale of personal property that is part of a real estate transaction when the terms of the sale are part of the real estate sales contract. *Note*: If you are at all unsure of the correct use of any forms in this chapter, please consult a competent attorney.

The following forms are provided in this section:

Contract for Sale of Personal Property: This form may be used for documenting the sale of any type of personal property. It may be used for vehicles, business assets, or any other personal property. The information necessary to complete this form are the names and addresses of the seller and the buyer, a complete description of the property being sold, the total purchase price, and the terms of the payment of this price.

Bill of Sale, with Warranties: This document is used as a receipt of the sale of personal property. It is, in many respects, often used to operate as a *title* (or ownership document) to items of personal property. It verifies that the person noted in the bill of sale has obtained legal title to the property from the previous owner. This particular version also provides that the seller *warrants* (or guarantees) that he or she has the authority to transfer legal title to the buyer and that there are no outstanding debts or liabilities for the property. In addition, this form provides that the seller warrants that the property is in good working condition on the date of the sale. To complete this form, simply fill in the names and addresses of the seller and buyer, the purchase price of the item, and a description of the property.

Bill of Sale, without Warranties: This form also provides a receipt to the buyer for the purchase of an item of personal property. However, in this form, the seller makes no warranties at all, either regarding the authority to sell the item or the condition of the item. It is sold to the buyer in "as is" condition. The buyer takes it regardless of any defects. To complete this form, fill in the names and addresses of the seller and buyer, the purchase price of the item, and a description of the property.

Bill of Sale, Subject to Debt: This form also provides a receipt to the buyer for the purchase of an item of personal property. This form, however, provides that the property sold is subject to a certain prior debt. It verifies that the seller has obtained legal title to the property from the previous owner, but that the seller specifies that the property is sold subject to a certain debt which the buyer is to pay off. In addition, the buyer agrees to indemnify the seller regarding any liability on the debt. This particular bill of sale version also provides that the seller warrants that he or she has authority to transfer legal title to the buyer. In addition, this form provides that the owner warrants that the property is in good working condition on the date of the sale. To complete this form, fill in the names and addresses of the seller and buyer, the purchase price of the item, a description of the property, and a description of the debt.

Contract for Sale of Personal Property

This Contract is made on _____ , 20 _____ , between
_____ , Seller,
address:

and _____ , Buyer,
address:

1. The Seller agrees to sell to the Buyer, and the Buyer agrees to buy the following personal property:

2. The Buyer agrees to pay the Seller $ _____ for the property. The Buyer agrees to pay this purchase price in the following manner:

3. The Buyer will be entitled to possession of this property on
    _____ , 20 _____ .

4. The Seller represents that it has legal title to the property and full authority to sell the property. Seller also represents that the property is sold free and clear of all liens, indebtedness, or liabilities. Seller agrees to provide Buyer with a Bill of Sale for the property.

5. This Contract binds and benefits both the Buyer and Seller and any successors. This document, including any attachments, is the entire agreement between the Buyer and Seller. This agreement is governed by the laws of the State of _____ .

_____   _____
Signature of Seller   Signature of Buyer

_____   _____
Printed Name of Seller   Printed Name of Buyer

Bill of Sale, with Warranties

This Bill of Sale is made on _____ , 20 _____ , between
_____ , Seller,
address:

and _____ , Buyer,
address:

In exchange for the payment of $ _____ , received from the Buyer, the Seller sells and transfers possession of the following property to the Buyer:

The Seller warrants that it owns this property and that it has the authority to sell the property to the Buyer. Seller also warrants that the property is sold free and clear of all liens, indebtedness, or liabilities.

The Seller also warrants that the property is in good working condition as of this date.

Signed and delivered to the Buyer on the above date.

_____

Signature of Seller

_____

Printed Name of Seller

Bill of Sale, without Warranties

This Bill of Sale is made on _____ , 20 _____ , between
_____ , Seller,
address:

and _____ , Buyer,
address:

In exchange for the payment of $ _____ , received from the Buyer, the Seller sells and transfers possession of the following property to the Buyer:

The Seller disclaims any implied warranty of merchantability or fitness and the property is sold in its present condition, "as is."

Signed and delivered to the Buyer on the above date.

_____
Signature of Seller

_____
Printed Name of Seller

Bill of Sale, Subject to Debt

This Bill of Sale is made on _____ , 20 _____ , between
_____ , Seller,
address:

and _____ , Buyer,
address:

In exchange for the payment of $ _____ , received from the Buyer, the Seller sells and transfers possession of the following property to the Buyer:

The Seller warrants that it owns this property and that it has the authority to sell the property to the Buyer. Seller also states that the property is sold subject to the following debt:

The Buyer buys the property subject to the above debt and agrees to pay the debt. Buyer also agrees to indemnify and hold the Seller harmless from any claim based on failure to pay off this debt.

The Seller also warrants that the property is in good working condition as of this date.

Signed and delivered to the Buyer on the above date.

_____   _____
Signature of Seller   Signature of Buyer

_____   _____
Printed Name of Seller   Printed Name of Buyer

CHAPTER 15
Sale of Real Estate

In this chapter are various forms for the sale and transfer of real estate. Although most real estate sales today are handled by real estate professionals, it is still perfectly legal to buy and sell property without the use of a real estate broker or lawyer. The forms provided in this chapter allow an individual to prepare the necessary forms for many basic real estate transactions. Please note, however, that there may be various state and local variations on sales contracts, mortgages, or other real estate documents. If in doubt, please check with a local real estate professional or an attorney. *Note*: If you are at all unsure of the correct use of any forms in this chapter, please consult a competent attorney. The following forms are provided:

Agreement to Sell Real Estate: This form may be used for setting down an agreement to buy and sell property. It contains the basic clauses to cover situations that will arise in most typical real estate transactions. The following items are covered:

- The sale is contingent on the buyer being able to obtain financing 30 days prior to the closing
- If the sale is not completed, the buyer will be given back the earnest money deposit, without interest or penalty
- The seller will provide a Warranty Deed for the real estate and a Bill of Sale for any personal property included in the sale
- Certain items will be pro-rated and adjusted as of the closing date
- The buyer and the seller may split the various closing costs
- The seller discloses and the buyer acknowledges any known lead-based paint in the building
- The seller represents that he or she has good title to the property and that the personal property included is in good working order
- The title to the property will be verified by either title insurance or an abstract of title

In order to prepare this contract, the following information will be necessary:

- The names and addresses of the buyer and seller
- A description of the property involved
- The purchase price of the property
- How the purchase price will be paid

- The amount of earnest money paid on signing the contract
- The date, place, and time for closing the sale
- What documents will be required at closing
- Which items will be adjusted and pro-rated at closing
- Which closing costs will be paid for by the seller and which costs by the buyer
- Whether there are any outstanding claims, liabilities, or indebtedness pertaining to the property
- Seller's disclosure and buying acknowledgment of lead-based paint
- Whether there are any additional terms
- Which state's laws will be used to interpret the contract

Title insurance or an abstract of title will need to be obtained from a local title company or attorney. Finally, a Bill of Sale for any personal property (Chapter 14: *Sale of Personal Property*) and a Warranty Deed will need to be prepared for use at the closing of the sale. In addition, a lead warning brochure may be required. This brochure can be downloaded at www.epa.gov/lead/leadpdfe.pdf

Option to Buy Real Estate Agreement: This form is designed to be used to offer an interested buyer a time period in which to have an exclusive option to purchase a parcel of real estate. It should be used in conjunction with a filled-in, but unsigned, copy of the above Contract for the Sale of Real Estate. Through the use of this agreement, the seller can offer the buyer a time in which to consider the purchase without concern of a sale to another party.

This agreement provides that in exchange for a payment (that will be applied to the purchase price if the option is exercised), the buyer is given a period of time to accept the terms of a completed real estate contract. If the buyer accepts the terms and exercises the option in writing, the seller agrees to complete the sale. If the option is not exercised, the seller is then free to sell the property on the market and retain the money paid for the option.

To complete this form, you will need the following information:

- The names and addresses of the buyer and seller
- A description of the property involved
- The amount of money to be paid for the option
- The time limit of the option
- The purchase price of the property

In addition, an Agreement to Sell Real Estate covering the property subject to the option should be completed and attached to the option agreement. This attached contract will provide all of the essential terms of the actual agreement to sell the property.

Quitclaim Deed: Any transfers of real estate must be in writing. This type of deed is intended to be used when the seller is merely selling whatever interest he or she may have in the property. By using a quitclaim deed, a seller is not, in any way, guaranteeing that he or she actually owns any interest in the property. This type of deed may be used to settle any claims that a person may have to a piece of real estate, to settle disputes over property, or to transfer property between co-owners.

To prepare this deed, simply fill in the names and addresses of the *grantor* (the one transferring the property) and the *grantee* (the one receiving the property) and the legal description of the property. For this deed form to be recorded, it must be properly notarized.

Warranty Deed: This type of deed is used in most real estate situations. It provides that the seller is *conveying* (transferring) to the buyer a full and complete title to the land without any restrictions or debts (a *fee simple* title). If there are any restrictions or debts that the property will be subject to, these should be noted in the legal description area provided.

To complete this deed, simply fill in the names and addresses of the *grantor* (the one selling the property) and the *grantee* (the one buying the property) and the legal description of the property. For the transfer to actually take place, the grantor must give the actual deed to the grantee. In addition, in order for this document to be recorded, it should be properly notarized.

Affidavit of Title: This specialized type of affidavit is used in real estate transactions to verify certain information regarding a piece of property. An Affidavit of Title is often required by a mortgage lender prior to approving a mortgage. With an Affidavit of Title, a landowner or seller states, under oath, that they have full possession and ownership of the property being sold. They also state the existence of any liens or claims against the property and that they have full authority to sell the property.

The information necessary for filling in this form are the name and address of the seller of the property, a complete legal description of the property, and a description of any liens or claims against the property. This form should be notarized as it may be required to be recorded.

Deed of Trust: A Deed of Trust is a document that creates a security interest in a parcel of property. It is similar to a *mortgage* (explained on the next page). It does not create the debt itself and so must be used in conjunction with a Promissory Note (Chapter 17: *Promissory Notes*). Some states use mortgages for this purpose and some states entitle such documents "deeds of trust." The purpose of both is the same. This document must be notarized and recorded in the land records office of the county where the property is located in order to be effective. Because of the many local and state variations in these type of documents, this document is for informational purposes only. *Note*: You are strongly advised to consult an attorney or real estate professional for information regarding preparation of a locally-acceptable deed of trust.

Mortgage: A mortgage is also a document that creates a security interest in a parcel of property, similar to a Deed of Trust. It does not create the debt itself and so must be used in conjunction with a Promissory Note (Chapter 17: *Promissory Notes*). Some states use mortgages for this purpose while other states refer to such documents as "deeds of trust." The purpose of both is the same: to create a security interest in the real estate. This document must be notarized and recorded in the land records office of the county where the property is located in order to be effective. Because of the many local and state variations in these type of documents, this document is provided here for informational purposes only.

Note: You are strongly advised to consult an attorney or real estate professional for information regarding preparation of a locally-acceptable mortgage.

Agreement to Sell Real Estate

This Agreement is made on _____ , 20 _____ , between
_____ , Seller,
address:

and _____ , Buyer,
address:

The Seller now owns the following described real estate, located at
_____ ,
City of _____ , State of _____ :

For valuable consideration, the Seller agrees to sell and the Buyer agrees to buy this property for the following price and on the following terms:

1. The Seller will sell this property to the Buyer, free from all claims, liabilities, and indebtedness, unless noted in this agreement.

2. The following personal property is also included in this sale:

3. The Buyer agrees to pay the Seller the sum of $ _____ , which the Seller agrees to accept as full payment. This agreement, however, is conditional upon the Buyer being able to arrange suitable financing on the following terms at least thirty (30) days prior to the closing date for this agreement: A mortgage in the amount of $ _____ , payable in _____ monthly payments, with an annual interest rate of _____ percent.

4. The purchase price will be paid as follows:
    Earnest deposit .... $ _____
    Other deposit: .... $ _____
    Cash or certified check on closing .... $ _____
    (subject to any adjustments or prorations on closing)

    Total Purchase Price .... $ _____

5. The Seller acknowledges receiving the earnest money deposit of $ _____ from the Buyer. If Buyer fails to perform this agreement, the Seller shall retain this money. If Seller fails to perform this agreement, this money shall be returned to the Buyer or the Buyer may have the right of specific performance. If Buyer is unable to obtain suitable financing at least thirty (30) days prior to closing, then this money will be returned to the Buyer without penalty or interest.

6. This agreement will close on _____ , 20 _____ , at _____ o'clock ____ . m., at _____ ,
    City of _____ , State of _____ . At that time, and upon payment by the Buyer of the portion of the purchase price then due, the Seller will deliver to Buyer the following documents:

    (a) A Bill of Sale for all personal property
    (b) A Warranty Deed for the real estate
    (c) A Seller's Affidavit of Title
    (d) A closing statement
    (e) Other documents:

7. At closing, pro-rated adjustments to the purchase price will be made for the following items:

    (a) Utilities
    (b) Property taxes
    (c) The following other items:

8. The following closing costs will be paid by the Seller:

9. The following closing costs will be paid by the Buyer:

10. Seller represents that it has good and marketable title to the property and will supply the Buyer with either an abstract of title or a standard policy of title insurance. Seller further represents that the property is free and clear of any restrictions on transfer, claims, indebtedness, or liabilities except the following:

    (a) Zoning, restrictions, prohibitions, or requirements imposed by any governmental authority
    (b) Any restrictions appearing on the plat of record of the property
    (c) Public utility easements of record
    (d) Other:

    Seller warrants that there shall be no violations of zoning or building codes as of the date of closing. Seller also warrants that all personal property included in this sale will be delivered in working order on the date of closing.

11. At least thirty (30) days prior to closing, Buyer shall have the right to obtain a written report from a licensed termite inspector stating that there is no termite infestation or termite damage to the property. If there is such evidence, Seller shall remedy such infestation and/or repair such damage, up to a maximum cost of two (2) percent of the purchase price of the property. If the costs exceed two (2) percent of the purchase price and Seller elects not to pay for the costs over two (2) percent, Buyer may cancel this agreement and the escrow shall be returned to Buyer without penalty or interest.

12. At least thirty (30) days prior to closing, Buyer or their agent shall have the right to inspect all heating, air conditioning, electrical, and mechanical systems of the property, the roof and all structural components of the property, and any personal property included in this agreement. If any such systems or equipment are not in working order, Seller shall pay for the cost of placing them in working order prior to closing. Buyer or their agent may again inspect the property withing forty-eight (48) hours of closing to determine if all systems and equipment are in working order.

13. Between the date of this agreement and the date for closing, the property shall be maintained in the condition as existed on the date of this agreement. If there is any damage by fire, casualty, or otherwise, prior to closing, Seller shall restore the property to the condition as existed on the date of this agreement. If Seller fails to do so, Buyer may:

(a) accept the property, as is, along with any insurance proceeds due Seller, *or*

(b) cancel this agreement and have the escrow deposit returned, without penalty or interest.

14. As required by law, the Seller makes the following statement: "Radon gas is a naturally occurring radioactive gas that, when accumulated in sufficient quantities in a building, may present health risks to persons exposed to it. Levels of radon gas that exceed federal and state guidelines have been found in buildings in this state. Additional information regarding radon gas and radon gas testing may be obtained from your county health department."

15. As required by law, the Seller makes the following *Lead Warning Statement*: "Every purchaser of any interest in residential real property on which a residential dwelling was built prior to 1978 is notified that such property may present exposure to lead from lead-based paint that may place young children at risk of developing lead poisoning. Lead poisoning in young children may produce permanent neurological damage, including learning disabilities, reduced intelligence quotient, behavioral problems, and impaired memory. Lead poisoning also poses a particular threat to pregnant women. The Seller of any interest in residential real estate is required to provide the Buyer with any information on lead-based paint hazards from risk assessments or inspection in the Seller's possession and notify the Buyer of any known lead-based paint hazards. A risk assessment or inspection for possible lead-based paint hazards is recommended prior to purchase."

Seller's Disclosure

Presence of lead-based paint and/or lead-based paint hazards: (Seller to initial one).

_____ Known lead-based paint and/or lead-based paint hazards are present in building (explain):

_____ Seller has no knowledge of lead-based paint and/or lead-based paint hazards in building.

Records and reports available to seller: (Seller to initial one).

_____ Seller has provided Buyer with all available records and reports pertaining to lead-based paint and/or lead-based paint hazards are present in building (list documents):

_____ Seller has no records and reports pertaining to lead-based paint and/or lead-based paint hazards in building.

Buyer's Acknowledgment

(Buyer to initial all applicable).

_____ Buyer has received copies of all information listed above.

_____ Buyer has received the pamphlet "Protect Your Family From Lead in Your Home."

_____ Buyer has received a ten (10)-day opportunity (or mutually-agreed on period) to conduct a risk assessment or inspection for the presence of lead-based paint and/or lead-based paint hazards in building.

_____ Buyer has waived the opportunity to conduct a risk assessment or inspection for the presence of lead-based paint and/or lead-based paint hazards in building.

The Seller and Buyer have reviewed the information above and certify, by their signatures at the end of this agreement, that to the best of their knowledge, the information they have provided is true and accurate.

16. The parties also agree to the following additional terms:

17. No modification of this agreement will be effective unless it is in writing and is signed by both the Buyer and Seller. This agreement binds and benefits both the Buyer and Seller and any successors. Time is of the essence of this agreement. This document, including any attachments, is the entire agreement between the Buyer and Seller. This agreement is governed by the laws of the State of _____ .

_____
Signature of Seller

_____
Printed Name of Seller

_____
Signature of Witness for Seller

_____
Printed Name of Witness for Seller

_____
Signature of Witness for Seller

_____
Printed Name of Witness for Seller

_____
Signature of Buyer

_____
Printed Name of Buyer

_____
Signature of Witness for Buyer

_____
Printed Name of Witness for Buyer

_____
Signature of Witness for Buyer

_____
Printed Name of Witness for Buyer

Option to Buy Real Estate Agreement

This Agreement is made on _____ , 20 _____ , between
_____ , Seller,
address:

and _____ , Buyer,
address:

The Seller now owns the following described real estate, located at
_____ ,
City of _____ , State of _____ :

For valuable consideration, the Seller agrees to give the Buyer an exclusive option to buy this property for the following price and on the following terms:

1. The Buyer will pay the Seller $ _____ for this option. This amount will be credited against the purchase price of the property if this option is exercised by the Buyer. If the option is not exercised, the Seller will retain this payment.

2. The option period will be from the date of this agreement until
_____ , 20 _____ , at which time the option provided by this agreement will expire unless exercised.

3. During this period, the Buyer has the option and exclusive right to buy the Seller's property mentioned above for the purchase price of $ _____ . The Buyer must notify the Seller, in writing, of the decision to exercise this option.

4. Attached to this Option to Buy Real Estate Agreement is a completed Contract for the Sale of Real Estate. If the Buyer notifies the Seller, in writing, of the decision to exercise the option within the option period, the Seller and Buyer agree to sign the contract for the sale of real estate and complete the sale on the terms contained in the contract.

5. No modification of this agreement will be effective unless it is in writing and is signed by both the Buyer and Seller. This agreement binds and benefits both the Buyer and Seller and any successors. Time is of the essence of this agreement. This document, including any attachments, is the entire agreement between the Buyer and Seller. This agreement is governed by the laws of the State of _____ .

_____
Signature of Seller

_____
Printed Name of Seller

_____
Signature of Buyer

_____
Printed Name of Buyer

Quitclaim Deed

This Quitclaim Deed is made on _____ , 20 _____ , between
_____ , Grantor,
address:

and _____ , Grantee,
address:

For valuable consideration, the Grantor hereby quitclaims and transfers the following described
real estate to the Grantee to have and hold forever, located at
_____ ,
City of _____ , State of _____ :

Dated: _____ , 20 _____

_____   _____
Signature of Grantor   Printed Name of Grantor

State of _____
County of _____

On _____ , 20 _____ , _____
personally came before me and, being duly sworn, did state that he or she is the person described in the above document and that he or she signed the above document in my presence.

_____
Signature of Notary Public

Notary Public, In and for the County of _____
State of _____

My commission expires: _____   Notary Seal

Warranty Deed

This Warranty Deed is made on _____ , 20 _____ , between
_____ , Grantor,
address:

and _____ , Grantee,
address:

For valuable consideration, the Grantor hereby sells, grants, and conveys the following described real estate, in fee simple, to the Grantee to have and hold forever, along with all easements, rights, and buildings belonging to the above property, located at
_____ ,
City of _____ , State of _____ :

The Grantor warrants that it is lawful owner and has full right to convey the property, and that the property is free from all claims, liabilities, or indebtedness, and that the Grantor and its successors will warrant and defend title to the Grantee against the lawful claims of all persons.

Dated: _____ , 20 _____

_____   _____
Signature of Grantor   Printed Name of Grantor

State of _____
County of _____

On _____ , 20 _____ , _____
personally came before me and, being duly sworn, did state that he or she is the person described in the above document and that he or she signed the above document in my presence.

_____
Signature of Notary Public

Notary Public, In and for the County of _____
State of _____

My commission expires: _____   Notary Seal

212

Affidavit of Title

This Affidavit of Title is made on _____ , 20 _____ , between
_____ , Seller,
address:

for _____ , Buyer,
address:

1. Seller certifies that it is now in possession of and is the absolute owner of the following property:

2. Seller also states that its possession has been undisputed and that Seller knows of no fact or reason that may prevent transfer of this property to the buyer.

3. Seller also states that no liens, contracts, debts, or lawsuits exist regarding this property, except the following:

4. Seller finally states that it has full power to transfer full title to this property to the buyer.

_____   _____

Signature of Seller   Printed Name of Seller

State of _____
County of _____

On _____ , 20 _____ , _____
personally came before me and, being duly sworn, did state that he or she is the person described in the above document and that he or she signed the above document in my presence.

_____

Signature of Notary Public

Notary Public, In and for the County of _____
State of _____

My commission expires: _____   Notary Seal

Deed of Trust

This Deed of Trust is made on _____ , 20 _____ , between
_____ , Grantor,
address:

and _____ , Grantee,
address:

1. For valuable consideration, the Grantor hereby grants the following described real estate
    to the Trustee in TRUST, along with all easements, rights, and buildings belonging to the
    above property, located at _____ ,
    City of _____ , State of _____ :

2. This Property is granted in TRUST to the Trustee to secure payment of the balance of the
    purchase price for the property owed to the Grantor by
    _____ Grantee,
    address:

3. The balance of the purchase price for this property is evidenced by a Promissory Note
    dated _____ , 20 _____ , in the principal amount of
    $ _____ , which is payable on or before _____ ,
    20 _____ , and bears interest at the annual rate of _____ percent, and which is pay-
    able to _____ , grantor
    address:

    A copy of the Promissory Note is attached and all of the terms of the note are made part
    of this document.

4. Upon evidence of full payment of the Promissory Note and satisfaction of all of the terms of the note, the Trustee shall deliver a signed Deed of Release to the Grantee.

Dated: _____ , 20 _____

_____   _____
Signature of Grantor   Printed Name of Grantor

State of _____
County of _____

On _____ , 20 _____ , _____
personally came before me and, being duly sworn, did state that he or she is the person described in the above document and that he or she signed the above document in my presence.

_____
Signature of Notary Public

Notary Public, In and for the County of _____
State of _____

My commission expires: _____   Notary Seal

Mortgage

This Mortgage is made on _____ , 20 _____ , between
_____ , Mortgagor,
address:

and _____ , Mortgagee,
address:

1. For valuable consideration, the Mortgagor hereby mortgages, grants, and conveys the
   following described real estate, in fee simple, to the Mortgagee to have and hold forever,
   along with all easements, rights, and buildings belonging to the above property, located
   at _____ ,
   City of _____ , State of _____ :

2. This Property is granted as security to the Mortgagee to secure payment of the balance of
   the purchase price for the property which is owed to the Mortgagee by the Mortgagor.

3. The balance of the purchase price for this property is evidenced by a promissory note
   dated _____ , 20 _____ , in the principal amount of
   $ _____ , which is payable on or before _____ ,
   20 _____ , and bears interest at the annual rate of _____ percent, and which is
   payable to Mortgagee. A copy of the Promissory Note is attached and all of the terms of
   the note are made part of this document.

4. Upon evidence of full payment of the promissory note and satisfaction of all of the terms
   of the note, the Mortgagee agrees to deliver a signed release of this mortgage to the Mortgagor.

5. The Mortgagor warrants that he or she is lawful owner and has full right to convey the property, and that the property is free from all claims, liabilities, or indebtedness, and that the Mortgagor, and his or her successors will warrant and defend title to the Mortgagee against the lawful claims of all persons.

Dated: _____ , 20 _____

_____   _____
Signature of Mortgagor   Printed Name of Mortgagor

State of _____
County of _____

On _____ , 20 _____ , _____
personally came before me and, being duly sworn, did state that he or she is the person described in the above document and that he or she signed the above document in my presence.

_____
Signature of Notary Public

Notary Public, In and for the County of _____
State of _____

My commission expires: _____   Notary Seal

CHAPTER 16
Personal Loan Documents

The documents included in this chapter are designed for use in situations in which a loan will be provided using personal property as collateral for the loan. Loans for real estate, other than a simple promissory note and mortgage or trust deed, are generally subject to more state regulations and, thus, should be handled by a real estate professional or attorney. The legal documents for financing of loans generally employ three key documents, each of which serves a different purpose. First, there is the actual *promissory note* by which the borrower promises to repay the debt. These documents are covered in Chapter 17: *Promissory Notes*. Next is the *security agreement* by which the borrower puts up specific property as collateral for repayment of the loan. Finally, there is the *U.C.C. financing statement* that is used to record the lien against the personal property in the public records.

All states have adopted a version of the Uniform Commercial Code (U.C.C.). This code is a set of detailed regulations which govern the purchase and sale of goods, and financing arrangements, along with many other commercial transactions. Every state has a method of filing (on the public record) various statements relating to financing arrangements. The value of making timely filings of financing statements and other U.C.C.-related matter is that the date and time of filing the statement *perfects* (or legally locks in time) the security interest that has been bargained for. The party with the earliest perfected security interest relating to a particular piece of property has priority claim to that property. *Note*: If you are at all unsure of the correct use of any forms in this chapter, please consult a competent attorney.

The various forms included in this chapter are as follows:

Security Agreement: This document is the document that provides the *secured party* (the party providing the loan) with the right to the collateral that the borrower has put up as security for the repayment of the loan.

The security agreement in this book provides for the following terms:

- The borrower is granting the secured party a security interest in the property named
- The security interest is to secure payment of a certain obligation
- If the borrower defaults on the obligation, the secured party may accelerate the loan and make it immediately due and payable

218

- If the borrower defaults, the secured party will have all the remedies under the U.C.C. (these may include selling the property or keeping the property)
- The borrower will pay any costs of collection upon default
- The borrower will be careful with the collateral and will not sell or dispose of it
- The borrower will insure the collateral and keep it at a specified address for the term of the loan period
- The borrower states that the property is owned free and clear, with no other liens against it, and that they have authority to use it as collateral
- The borrower will sign any necessary financing statements
- Any changes to the agreement must be in writing

Receipt for Collateral: If it is desired that the property offered as collateral be held by the secured party, it will be necessary to alter the above Security Agreement by deleting Paragraphs 5 and 6 and preparing this receipt for the collateral. This receipt provides:

- The secured party has obtained the collateral and will hold it as security until the loan is repaid
- If the borrower defaults on the obligation, the property may be disposed of to satisfy the obligation
- The borrower will pay any costs and expenses relating to holding the property
- The secured party does not acknowledge the value or condition of the property offered as collateral

U.C.C. Financing Statement: This form is a memorandum of the details of a security arrangement. It is designed to be filed with the appropriate state filing office in order to record the security interest. Once filed, this statement serves as a public record of the date and time that the security interest in the particular property was perfected. To fill in this form, simply provide the namese and addresses of the parties and a description of the security interest being filed.

Release of U.C.C. Financing Statement: This form is a memorandum detailing the release of the financing obligation and should be filed with the state filing office to clear the records once the obligation has been satisfied. To fill in this form, simply provide the names and addresses of the parties and a description of the financing statement being released.

Release of Security Interest: This form acts as a release of the property from its *nature* (or use) as collateral for the loan. In addition, when the loan is repaid, the promissory note or obligation should also be released (see Chapter 17: *Promissory Notes*). To fill in this form, simply provide the names and addresses of the parties and a description of the security interest being released.

Security Agreement

This Agreement is made on _____ , 20 _____ , between
_____ , Borrower,
address:

and _____ , Secured Party,
address:

For valuable consideration, the parties agree as follows:

1. The Borrower grants the Secured Party a security interest under Article 9 of the Uniform Commercial Code (U.C.C.) in the following personal property which will be considered collateral:

2. This security interest is granted to secure payment by the Borrower to the Secured Party on the following obligation:

3. In the event of default by the Borrower in payment of any of the amounts due on the obligation listed under Paragraph 2, the Secured Party may declare the entire obligation immediately due and payable and will have all of the remedies of a secured party under the Uniform Commercial Code.

4. In the event of such default, Borrower will also be responsible for any costs of collection, including court costs and attorney fees.

5. The Borrower agrees to use reasonable care in using the collateral and agrees not to sell or dispose of the collateral.

6. The Borrower agrees to keep the collateral adequately insured and at the following address for the entire term of this security agreement:

7. The Borrower represents that the collateral is owned free and clear and that there are no other security agreements, indebtedness, or liens relating to the property offered as collateral. Borrower also states that it has full authority to grant this security interest.

8. Borrower agrees to sign any financing statements that are required by the Secured Party to perfect this security interest.

9. No modification of this agreement will be effective unless it is in writing and is signed by both parties. This agreement binds and benefits both parties and any successors.

10. Time is of the essence of this agreement. This document, including any attachments, is the entire agreement between the parties. This agreement is governed by the laws of the State of _____ .

The parties have signed this agreement on the date specified at the beginning of this agreement.

_____
Signature of Borrower

_____
Printed Name of Borrower

_____
Signature of Secured Party

_____
Printed Name of Secured Party

Receipt for Collateral

This receipt is made in connection with the promissory note dated
_____ , 20 _____ , and the security agreement dated
_____ , 20 _____ , between
_____ , Borrower,
address:

and _____ , Noteholder/ Secured Party,
address:

The Noteholder/Secured Party acknowledges delivery of the following described personal property as collateral under the security agreement:

This collateral is subject to the lien and all of the conditions of the security agreement. In the event of the Borrower's default on any of the terms of the note or security agreement, this property may be disposed of by the Noteholder/Secured Party to satisfy any of the Borrower's obligations as allowed by law.

The Borrower will continue to pay all costs and expenses relating to this property, including any maintenance, storage fees, insurance, or taxes.

This receipt does not acknowledge the condition or the value of the property retained as collateral.

Dated: _____ , 20 _____

_____
Signature of Borrower

_____
Printed Name of Borrower

_____
Signature of Noteholder/Secured Party

_____
Printed Name of Noteholder/Secured Party

U.C.C. Financing Statement

This original Financing Statement is presented for filing under the U.C.C. (Uniform Commercial Code) as adopted in the following State of _____ .

(This section for use of the filing officer)

Date of filing _____ , 20 _____   Time of filing _____

Number of filing office _____

Address of filing office:

Name(s) of Borrower _____

Address(es) of Borrower:

Name(s) of Secured Party _____

Address(es) of Secured Party:

This financing statement covers the following personal property:

This financing statement secures a debt document described as:

Name of document _____

Date of document _____ , 20 _____

Face value of document $ _____   Maturity date _____ , 20 _____

Related terms and conditions of the debt are contained in this debt document and any other documents mentioned in the debt document.

Dated: _____ , 20 _____   Seal

_____   _____
Signature of Borrower   Printed Name of Borrower

Release of U.C.C. Financing Statement

This Release of Financing Statement is presented for filing under the U.C.C. (Uniform Commercial Code) as adopted in the following State of _____ .

(This section for use of the filing officer)

Date of filing _____ , 20 _____ Time of filing _____

Number of filing office _____

Address of filing office:

Name(s) of Borrower _____

Address(es) of Borrower:

Name(s) of Secured Party _____

Address(es) of Secured Party:

The original financing statement covers the following personal property:

File # of original Financing Statement: _____

Date of filing of original Financing Statement: _____

Number of office where original Financing Statement was filed _____

Address of office where original Financing Statement was filed:

224

Dated: _____ , 20 _____   Seal

_____   _____
Signature of Secured Party   Printed Name of Secured Party

State of _____
County of _____

On _____ , 20 _____ , _____
personally came before me and, being duly sworn, did state that he or she is the person described in the above document and that he or she signed the above document in my presence.

_____
Signature of Notary Public

Notary Public, In and for the County of _____
State of _____

My commission expires: _____   Notary Seal

Release of Security Interest

For valuable consideration,

_____ , Secured Party,
address:

releases _____ , Borrower,
address:

from the following specific security agreement, dated: _____ :

Any claims or obligations that not specifically mentioned are not released by this release of security interest.

The Secured Party has not assigned any claims or obligations covered by this release to any other party.

The Secured Party will sign a release of U.C.C. financing statement if requested by Borrower.

The party signing this release intends that it both bind and benefit any successors.

Dated: _____ , 20 _____

_____   _____
Signature of Secured Party   Printed Name of Secured Party

_____   _____
Signature of Borrower   Printed Name of Borrower

CHAPTER 17
Promissory Notes

Contained in this chapter are various promissory notes. A *promissory note* is a document by which a borrower promises to pay the holder of the note a certain amount of money under specific terms. In the forms in this chapter, the person who borrows the money is referred to as the *borrower* and the person whom the borrower is to pay is referred to as the *noteholder*. The noteholder is generally also the lender, but this need not be so. The forms in this chapter are intended for use only by individuals who are not regularly in the business of lending money. Complex state and federal regulations apply to lending institutions and such rules are beyond the scope of this book. This chapter also contains various forms for demanding payments on a promissory note. *Note*: If you are at all unsure of the correct use of any forms in this chapter, please consult a competent attorney.

Promissory Note (Installment Repayment): This type of promissory note is a standard unsecured note. Being *unsecured* means that the noteholder has no collateral or specific property to foreclose against should the borrower default on the note. If the borrower doesn't pay, the noteholder must sue and get a general judgment against the borrower. Collection of the judgment may then be made against the borrower's assets.

This particular note calls for the borrower to pay a certain annual interest rate on the note and to make periodic payments to the noteholder. It also has certain general terms:

- The borrower may prepay any amount on the note without penalty
- If the borrower is in default, the noteholder may demand full payment on the note
- The note is not assumable by anyone other than the borrower
- The borrower waives certain formalities relating to demands for payment
- The borrower agrees to pay any of the costs of collection after a default

In order to complete this form, the following information is necessary:

- The names and addresses of the borrower and the noteholder
- The amount of the principal of the loan
- The annual interest rate to be charged
- The period for the installments (for example, monthly or weekly)
- The date of the period on which payments will be due
- The number of days a payment may be late before it is considered a default

Promissory Note (Lump Sum Repayment): This note is also an unsecured promise to pay. However, this version of a promissory note calls for the payment, including accrued interest, to be paid in one lump sum at a certain date in the future. This note has the same general conditions relating to prepayment, defaults, and assumability as the Promissory Note with Installment Payments discussed on the previous page.

To prepare this form, use the following information:

- The names and addresses of the borrower and the noteholder
- The amount of the principal of the loan
- The annual interest rate to be charged
- The final due date of the lump sum payment
- The number of days past the due date that payment may be made before the note is in default

Promissory Note (on Demand): This also is an unsecured note. This type of promissory note, however, is immediately payable in full at any time upon the demand of the noteholder. This note has the same general conditions relating to prepayment, defaults, and assumability as the Promissory Note with Installment Payments discussed previously.

The following information is necessary to complete this form:

- The names and addresses of the borrower and the noteholder
- The amount of the principal of the loan
- The annual interest rate to be charged
- The number of days past the demand date that payment may be made before the note is in default

Promissory Note (Secured): This type of promissory note is referred to as a *secured* note. What this means is that the borrower has given the noteholder some form of property or right to property as collateral for the loan. This allows the noteholder a direct claim against the specific property and the ability to foreclose against the property if the note is in default. A secured note also places the noteholder higher on the list for repayment if the borrower files for bankruptcy.

This particular form is designed to be used in conjunction with a completed Security Agreement (Chapter 16: *Personal Loan Documents*) covering the security arrangement between the borrower and the noteholder (lender). The security for this type of note must be personal property. A secured promissory note may be drawn up for use with real estate as collateral. However, since this will entail the use of a mortgage or deed of trust as the security agreement, the services of a lawyer or real estate professional may be required. This secured promissory note is set up for installment payments.

However, the language from a "demand" or "lump-sum" payment-type note can be substituted, if desired.

The conditions of this promissory note are as follows:

- Default on any of the conditions of the underlying security agreement may allow the noteholder to demand immediate full payment on the note
- The borrower may prepay any amount on the note without penalty
- If the borrower is in default, the noteholder may demand full payment on the note
- The note is not assumable by anyone other than the borrower
- The borrower waives certain formalities relating to demands for payment
- The borrower agrees to pay any of the costs of collection after a default

The following information is needed to complete this form:

- The names and addresses of the borrower and the noteholder
- The amount of the principal of the loan
- The annual interest rate to be charged
- The period for the installments (for example, monthly or weekly)
- The date of the period on which payments will be due
- The date of the security agreement which coincides with the note
- The number of days a payment may be late before it is considered a default

Release of Promissory Note: This release is intended to be used to release a party from obligations under a Promissory Note. There are several other methods by which to accomplish this same objective. The return of the original note to the maker, clearly marked "Paid in Full" will serve the same purpose. A Receipt in Full will also accomplish this goal (see Chapter 10: *Releases*). The Release of Promissory Note may, however, be used in those situations when the release is based on something other than payment in full of the underlying note. For example, the note may be satisfied by a gift from the bearer of the note of release from the obligation. Another situation may involve a release of the note based on a concurrent release of a claim that the maker of the note holds against the holder of the note.

Demand and Notice of Default on Installment Promissory Note: This form will be used to notify the maker of a promissory note of his or her default on an installment payment on a promissory note. Notice of default should be sent promptly to any account that falls behind in its payments on a note. This promissory note provides a legal basis for a suit for breach of the promissory note.

Demand and Notice for Full Payment on Installment Promissory Note: A demand for full payment on a promissory note can be made only if the precise terms of the note allow for this. A note may have specific terms that allow it to be accelerated upon default on any payments. This means that if the maker of the note falls behind on his or her payments, the holder may *accelerate* all of the payment dates to the present and demand that the note be paid in full. Generally, this form will be used after giving the debtor a reasonable time to make up the missed installment payment.

Demand and Notice for Payment on Demand Promissory Note: This document should be used when you hold a promissory note that is payable on demand and you wish to demand full payment. Realistically, you should generally allow the maker of such a note a reasonable time to gather enough funds to make the payment. This form allows a period of 10 days. However, you may wish to modify this period after consulting with the debtor.

Promissory Note (Installment Repayment)

$ _____

Dated: _____ , 20 _____

For value received,

_____ , Borrower,

address:

promises to pay

_____ , Noteholder,

address:

the principal amount of $ _____ , with interest at the annual rate of _____ per-
cent, on any unpaid balance.

Payments are payable to the Noteholder in _____ consecutive installments
of $ _____ , including interest, and continuing on the _____ day of each
_____ until paid in full. If not paid off sooner, this note is due and payable in full
on _____ , 20 _____ .

This note may be prepaid in whole or in part at any time without penalty. If the Borrower
is in default more than _____ days with any payment, this note is payable
upon demand of any Noteholder. This note is not assumable without the written consent of
the Noteholder. The Borrower waives demand, presentment for payment, protest, and notice.
In the event of any default, the Borrower will be responsible for any costs of collection on
this note, including court costs and attorney fees.

_____

Signature of Borrower

_____

Printed Name of Borrower

Promissory Note (Lump Sum Repayment)

$ _____

Dated: _____ , 20 _____

For value received,

_____ , Borrower,
address:

promises to pay

_____ , Noteholder,
address:

the principal amount of $ _____ , with interest at the annual rate of _____ per-
cent, on any unpaid balance.

Payment on this note is due and payable to the Noteholder in full on or before
_____ , 20 _____ .

This note may be prepaid in whole or in part at any time without penalty. If the Borrower
is in default more than _____ days with any payment, this note is payable
upon demand of any Noteholder. This note is not assumable without the written consent of
the Noteholder. The Borrower waives demand, presentment for payment, protest, and notice.
In the event of any default, the Borrower will be responsible for any costs of collection on
this note, including court costs and attorney fees.

_____
Signature of Borrower

_____
Printed Name of Borrower

Promissory Note (on Demand)

$ _____

Dated: _____ , 20 _____

For value received,

_____ , Borrower,

address:

promises to pay ON DEMAND to

_____ , Noteholder,

address:

the principal amount of $ _____ , with interest at the annual rate of _____ percent, on any unpaid balance.

This note may be prepaid in whole or in part at any time without penalty. This note is not assumable without the written consent of the Noteholder. The Borrower waives demand, presentment for payment, protest, and notice. In the event of such default of over _____ days in making payment, the Borrower will be also be responsible for any costs of collection on this note, including court costs and attorney fees.

_____
Signature of Borrower

_____
Printed Name of Borrower

Promissory Note (Secured)

$ _____

Dated: _____ , 20 _____

For value received,

_____ , Borrower,

address:

promises to pay

_____ , Noteholder,

address:

the principal amount of $ _____ , with interest at the annual rate of _____ per-
cent, on any unpaid balance.

Payments are payable to the Noteholder in _____ consecutive installments
of $ _____ , including interest, and continuing on the _____ day of each
_____ until paid in full. If not paid off sooner, this note is due and payable in full
on _____ , 20 _____ .

This note is secured by a security agreement dated _____ ,
20 _____ , which has also been signed by the Borrower. This note may be accelerated and
demand for immediate full payment made by the Noteholder upon breach of any conditions
of the security agreement. This note may be prepaid in whole or in part at any time without
penalty. If the Borrower is in default more than _____ days with any payment,
this note is payable upon demand of any Noteholder. This note is not assumable without the
written consent of the Noteholder. The Borrower waives demand, presentment for payment,
protest, and notice. In the event of any default, the Borrower will be responsible for any costs
of collection on this note, including court costs and attorney fees.

_____

Signature of Borrower

_____

Printed Name of Borrower

Release of Promissory Note

In consideration of full payment of the promissory note dated
_____ , 20 _____ , in the face amount of $ _____ ,
_____ , Noteholder,
address:

releases and discharges
_____ , Borrower(s),
address:

from any claims or obligations on account of this note.

The party signing this release intends that it bind and benefit both itself and any successors.

Dated: _____ , 20 _____

_____
Signature of Noteholder

_____
Printed Name of Noteholder

Demand and Notice of Default on Installment Promissory Note

Date: _____ , 20 _____

To: _____

RE: Default on Installment Promissory Note

Dear _____ :

Regarding the promissory note dated _____ , 20 _____ , in the original amount of $ _____ , of which you are the maker, you have defaulted on the installment payment due on _____ , 20 _____ , in the amount of $ _____ .

Demand is made upon you for payment of this past-due installment payment. If payment is not received by us within ten (10) days from the date of this notice, we will proceed to enforce our rights under the promissory note for collection of the entire balance.

Very truly,

_____
Signature of Noteholder

_____
Printed Name of Noteholder

Demand and Notice for Full Payment on Installment Promissory Note

Date: _____ , 20 _____

To: _____

RE: Full Payment on Installment Promissory Note

Dear _____ :

I am currently the holder of your promissory note dated _____ ,
20 _____ , in the amount of $ _____ , which is payable to
_____ , Noteholder
address and phone number:

You have been given previous notice on _____ , 20 _____ ,
of your default on payments of this note. Under the terms of the note and by this notice,
I am making a formal demand for payment by you of the full unpaid balance of this note,
together with all accrued interest within ten (10) days of receipt of this letter. Please contact me at the above address and phone number in order to initiate the payment process. If
full payment is not received within ten (10) days from the date of this demand, the note shall
be forwarded to our attorneys for legal collection proceedings and you will be immediately
liable for all costs of collection, including additional legal and court costs. Thank you very
much for your prompt attention to this serious matter.

Very truly,

_____
Signature of Noteholder

_____
Printed Name of Noteholder

Demand and Notice for Payment on Demand Promissory Note

Date: _____ , 20 _____

To: _____

RE: Payment on Demand Promissory Note

Dear _____ :

I am currently the holder of your promissory note dated _____ ,
20 _____ , in the amount of $ _____ , which is payable to
_____ , the original Noteholder, or
to _____ , the holder on demand.

By this notice, I am making a formal demand for payment by you of the full unpaid balance
of this note, together with all accrued interest, within ten (10) days of receipt of this letter.
The total amount due at this time is $ _____ .

Please contact me at the address and phone number below in order to initiate the payment
process. If full payment is not received within ten (10) days from the date of this demand,
the note shall be forwarded to our attorneys for legal collection proceedings and you will be
immediately liable for all costs of collection, including any additional legal and court costs.
Thank you very much for your prompt attention to this serious matter.

Very truly,

_____
Signature of Current Noteholder

_____
Printed Name of Current Noteholder

_____
Address of Current Noteholder

_____
Phone Number of Current Noteholder

CHAPTER 18
Collection Documents

The documents contained in this chapter are for use in the collection of past-due payments that are owed to you. Through the proper use of the documents in this chapter, you should be able to collect on the majority of overdue and unpaid accounts without having to resort to the use of attorneys or collection agencies. Of course, if the initial attempts at collection using these documents fail, then it is advisable to turn the accounts over to parties who will be able to bring legal procedures to bear on the defaulting parties. The following forms are included in this chapter:

Request for Payment: This form should be used to make the initial request for payment from an overdue payment. It should be sent when you have decided that a payment due is in delinquent status. It is intended to promote payment on the overdue account. To prepare it, you will need to enter: the name of the company or person with the delinquent payment; the date, amount, and invoice number of the past-due payment; any interest or late charges that have been assessed; and any credits or payments that have been made on the account. Be sure to keep a record of this request. Generally, making a copy of the actual request that is sent and placing it in the file for the overdue account is the easiest method.

Second Request for Payment: You will generally use this form about 30 days after you have sent the first request for payment. The information necessary for this form will be the same as the first request. You will, however, need to update any additions or subtractions to the account that have taken place during the period since the first request (for example: any payments on account, additional interest charges, additional late payments, etc.).

Final Demand for Payment: This form should normally be used after 30 more days have elapsed since the second payment request was sent. It is a notice that collection proceedings will be begun if payment has not been received on the delinquent account within 10 days. (Please note that you may extend this period if you desire, for example, to allow for 30 days to pay). This notice should not be sent unless you actually plan on following up with the collection. However, it is often reasonable to wait a short while after the deadline before proceeding with assignment of the account for collection. This allows for delays in mail delivery and takes into account the tendency of companies and people with debt problems to push the time limits to the maximum. Should this demand letter fail to produce any results, you are advised to seek the assistance of a competent attorney or a reputable collection agency.

Request for Payment

Date: _____ , 20 _____

To:_____

RE: Payment of Your Account

Dear _____ :

Regarding your loan, please be advised that we show the following outstanding balance on our books:

Invoice # _____   Date _____   Amount $ _____
Invoice # _____   Date _____   Amount $ _____
Interest on account at _____ percent   Amount $ _____
Late charges   Amount $ _____
Less credits and payments   Amount $ _____

TOTAL BALANCE DUE   AMOUNT $ _____

Please be advised that we have not yet received payment on this outstanding balance. We are certain that this is merely an oversight and would ask that you please send the payment now. Please disregard this notice if full payment has been forwarded to us.

Thank you for your immediate attention to this matter.

Very truly,

_____
Signature

_____
Printed Name

Second Request for Payment

Date: _____ , 20 _____

To: _____

RE: Payment of Your Account

Dear _____ :

Regarding your account, please be advised that we continue to show the following outstanding balance on our books:

Invoice # _____ Date _____ Amount $ _____
Invoice # _____ Date _____ Amount $ _____
Interest on account at _____ percent   Amount $ _____
Late charges   Amount $ _____
Less credits and payments   Amount $ _____

TOTAL BALANCE DUE   AMOUNT $ _____

Please be advised that since our last request for payment dated _____ , 20 _____ , we have still not yet received payment on this outstanding balance. We must request that you please send the payment immediately. Please disregard this notice if full payment has been forwarded to us.

Thank you for your immediate attention to this matter.

Very truly,

_____
Signature

_____
Printed Name

Final Demand for Payment

Date: _____ , 20 _____

To: _____

RE: Payment of Your Account

Dear _____ :

Regarding your delinquent account in the amount of $ _____ , we have requested payment on this account several times without success.

THIS IS YOUR FINAL NOTICE.

Please be advised that unless we receive payment in full on this account in this office within ten (10) days of the date of this letter, we will immediately turn this account over to our attorneys for collection proceedings against you without further notice.

These proceedings will include claims for pre-judgment interest on your account and all legal and court-related costs in connection with collection of this past-due account and will substantially increase the amount that you owe us. Collection proceedings may also have an adverse effect on your credit rating.

We regret the necessity for this action and urge you to clear up this account delinquency immediately. If full payment has been sent, please disregard this notice.

Thank you for your immediate attention to this serious matter.

Very truly,

_____
Signature

_____
Printed Name

CHAPTER 19
Miscellaneous Legal Forms

Included in this chapter are various documents that may be used in a variety of circumstances. These documents range from a form for making sworn statements to an indemnity agreement that can be used by a party to accept responsibility for any claims or liability that may arise in a transaction. *Note*: If you are at all unsure of the correct use of any forms in this chapter, please consult a competent attorney. The forms that are included and the information necessary to prepare them are as follows:

Affidavit: This document is a basic form for an affidavit. An *affidavit* is a legal document with which a person can make a sworn statement regarding anything. It is essentially testimony, under oath, by the person making the affidavit. An affidavit may be used to document an aspect of a business transaction. It may also be used as a supplement to a lawsuit. The information necessary to prepare the basic affidavit are the name and address of the person making the affidavit and a written recital of the statement that the person is affirming. This form should be notarized, as the statement is being made under oath and under penalty of perjury.

Independent Contractor Agreement: An *independent contractor* may also be hired to perform a job. As opposed to an *employee*, this type of worker is defined as one who maintains his or her own independent business, uses his or her own tools, and does not work under the direct supervision of the person who has hired him or her. This form should be used when hiring an independent contractor. It provides a standard form for the hiring out of specific work to be performed within a set time period for a particular payment. It also provides a method for authorizing extra work under the contract. Finally, this document provides that the contractor agrees to indemnify the owner against any claims or liabilities arising from the performance of the work.

To complete this form, fill in a detailed description of the work, dates by which portions of the job are to be completed, the pay for the job, the terms and dates of payment, and the state whose laws will govern the contract.

Request for Credit Information: This form is designed to be used to obtain information regarding your personal credit history from any credit reporting agency. It is in accordance with the Federal Fair Credit Reporting Act. Fill in the appropriate information and forward it to the credit reporting agency from which you wish to obtain information.

Notice of Disputed Account: This form should be used by you if you have received a statement with which you disagree. If you feel that the statement is in error, spell out your reasoning in the space provided and send this form to the creditor.

Stop Payment on Check Order: This form is intended to be provided to a bank or similar financial institution to confirm a telephone stop payment request. This form provides the institution with written confirmation of the oral request to stop payment on a check.

Request for Removal from Mailing List: This form may be used to notify a company that you wish to be removed from their mailing list and that you do not wish your name and address to be sold or given to any other party.

Affidavit

I,_____ ,
being of legal age, make the following statements and declare that, on my own personal knowledge, they are true:

Signed under the penalty of perjury on _____ , 20 _____ .

_____
Signature

_____
Printed Name

State of _____
County of _____

On _____ , 20 _____ , _____
personally came before me and, being duly sworn, did state that he or she is the person de-scribed in the above document and that he or she signed the above document in my presence.

_____
Signature of Notary Public

Notary Public, In and for the County of _____
State of _____

My commission expires: _____   Notary Seal

Independent Contractor Agreement

This Agreement is made on _____ , 20 _____ , between _____ , Owner, address:

and _____ , Contractor, address:

For valuable consideration, the Owner and Contractor agree as follows:

1. The Contractor agrees to furnish all of the labor and materials to do the following work for the Owner as an independent contractor:

2. The Contractor agrees that the following portions of the total work will be completed by the dates specified:

3. The Contractor agrees to perform this work in a workmanlike manner according to standard practices. If any plans or specifications are part of this job, they are attached to and are part of this contract.

4. The Owner agrees to pay the Contractor as full payment $ _____ , for doing the work outlined above. This price will be paid to the Contractor upon satisfactory completion of the work in the following manner and on the following dates:

5. The Contractor and Owner may agree to extra services and work, but any such extras must be set out and agreed to in writing by both the Contractor and the Owner.

6. The Contractor agrees to indemnify and hold the Owner harmless from any claims or liability arising from the Contractor's work under this contract.

7. No modification of this contract will be effective unless it is in writing and is signed by both parties. This contract binds and benefits both parties and any successors. Time is of the essence of this contract. This document, including any attachments, is the entire agreement between the parties. This contract is governed by the laws of the State of

_____ .

Dated: _____ , 20 _____

_____
Signature of Owner

_____
Printed Name of Owner

_____
Signature of Contractor

_____
Printed Name of Contractor

Request for Credit Information

To:_____

RE: Disclosure of Credit Information

By this letter, I hereby request complete disclosure of my personal credit file as held within your agency records. This request is in accordance with the Federal Fair Credit Reporting Act. I request that this disclosure provide the names and addresses of any parties who have received a copy of my credit report, and the names and addresses of any parties who have provided information that is contained in my credit report.

Name _____

Prior or other name _____

Address:

Prior or other address:

Social Security # _____   Phone _____

Dated: _____ , 20 _____

_____   _____
Signature   Printed Name

State of _____
County of _____

On _____ , 20 _____ , _____
personally came before me and, being duly sworn, did state that he or she is the person described in the above document and that he or she signed the above document in my presence.

_____
Signature of Notary Public

Notary Public, In and for the County of _____
State of _____

My commission expires: _____   Notary Seal

Notice of Disputed Account

Date: _____ , 20 _____

To: _____

RE: Disputed Account

Dear _____ :

We are in receipt of your statement of our account dated _____ ,
20 _____ , indicating a balance due you of $ _____ .

We dispute this amount due for the following reasons:

Please contact us immediately to discuss the adjustment of our account.

Very truly,

_____
Signature

_____
Printed Name

Stop Payment on Check Order

Date: _____ , 20 _____

To: _____

RE: Stop Payment on Check

Dear _____ :

Pursuant to our telephone conversation of _____ , 20 _____ ,
please stop payment on the following check:

Account name _____

Account # _____

Check # _____

Check date _____

Check amount _____

Payable to _____

Thank you for your immediate attention to this matter.

Very truly,

_____

Signature

_____

Printed Name

Request for Removal from Mailing List

Date: _____ , 20 _____

To: _____

RE: Removal from Mailing List

Dear _____ :

By this letter, I request that the following name please be removed from your mailing list:

I also request that my name and address not be sold or given to any other person or entity. Thank you for your immediate attention to this matter.

Very truly,

_____
Signature

_____
Printed Name

Index

✯ Nova Publishing Company ✯

Small Business and Consumer Legal Books and Software

Law Made Simple Series

Basic Wills Simplified

ISBN 0-935755-90-X	Book only	$22.95
ISBN 0-935755-89-6	Book w/Forms-on-CD	$28.95

Divorce Agreements Simplified

ISBN 0-935755-87-X	Book only	$24.95
ISBN 0-935755-86-1	Book w/Forms-on-CD	$29.95

Living Trusts Simplified

ISBN 0-935755-53-5	Book only	$22.95
ISBN 0-935755-51-9	Book w/Forms-on-CD	$28.95

Living Wills Simplified

ISBN 0-935755-52-7	Book only	$22.95
ISBN 0-935755-50-0	Book w/Forms-on-CD	$28.95

Personal Bankruptcy Simplified (available Summer 2004)

ISBN 0-892949-01-6	Book only	$22.95
ISBN 0-892949-02-4	Book w/Forms-on-CD	$28.95

Personal Legal Forms Simplified

ISBN 0-935755-97-7	Book w/Forms-on-CD	$28.95

Small Business Made Simple Series

Small Business Accounting Simplified (3rd Edition)

ISBN 0-935755-91-8	Book only	$22.95

Small Business Bookkeeping Systems Simplified

ISBN 0-935755-74-8	Book only	$14.95

Small Business Payroll Systems Simplified)

ISBN 0-935755-55-1	Book only	$14.95

Small Business Library Series

Incorporate Now!: The National Corporation Kit (Available Summer 2004)

ISBN 0-892949-00-8	Book w/Forms-on-CD	$28.95

The Complete Book of Small Business Legal Forms (3rd Edition)

ISBN 0-935755-84-5	Book w/Forms-on-CD	$24.95

The Complete Book of Small Business Management Forms

ISBN 0-935755-56-X	Book w/Forms-on-CD	$24.95

Small Business Start-up Series

C-Corporations: Small Business Start-up Kit

ISBN 0-935755-78-0	Book w/Forms-on-CD	$24.95

Limited Liability Company: Small Business Start-up Kit

ISBN 0-935755-76-4	Book w/Forms-on-CD	$24.95

Partnerships: Small Business Start-up Kit

ISBN 0-935755-75-6	Book w/Forms-on-CD	$24.95

S-Corporations: Small Business Start-up Kit

ISBN 0-935755-77-2	Book w/Forms-on-CD	$24.95

Sole Proprietorship: Small Business Start-up Kit

ISBN 0-935755-79-9	Book w/Forms-on-CD	$24.95

Legal Self-Help Series

Divorce Yourself: The National No-Fault Divorce Kit (5th Edition)

ISBN 0-935755-93-4	Book only	$24.95
ISBN 0-935755-94-2	Book w/Forms-on-CD	$34.95

Prepare Your Own Will: The National Will Kit (5th Edition)

ISBN 0-935755-72-1	Book only	$17.95
ISBN 0-935755-73-X	Book w/Forms-on-CD	$27.95

National Legal Kits

Simplified Bankruptcy Kit

ISBN 0-935755-83-7	*Book only*	*$17.95*

Simplified Divorce Kit

ISBN 0-935755-81-0	*Book only*	*$19.95*

Simplified Will Kit

ISBN 0-935755-96-9	*Book only*	*$16.95*

✯ Ordering Information ✯

Distributed by:
National Book Network
4501 Forbes Blvd. #200
Lanham MD 20706

Shipping: $4.50 for first & $.75 for each additional
Phone orders with Visa/MC: (800) 462-6420
Fax orders with Visa/MC: (800) 338-4550
Internet: www.novapublishing.com